T0155598

Practical GameMaker Projects

Build Games with GameMaker Studio 2

Ben Tyers

Apress®

Practical GameMaker Projects: Build Games with GameMaker Studio 2

Ben Tyers
Worthing, West Sussex, United Kingdom

ISBN-13 (pbk): 978-1-4842-3744-1   ISBN-13 (electronic): 978-1-4842-3745-8
https://doi.org/10.1007/978-1-4842-3745-8

Library of Congress Control Number: 2018950019

Managing Director, Apress Media LLC: Welmoed Spahr
Acquisitions Editor: Steve Anglin
Development Editor: Matthew Moodie
Coordinating Editor: Mark Powers

Cover designed by eStudioCalamar

Cover image designed by Freepik (www.freepik.com)

Distributed to the book trade worldwide by Springer Science+Business Media New York, 233 Spring Street, 6th Floor, New York, NY 10013. Phone 1-800-SPRINGER, fax (201) 348-4505, e-mail orders-ny@springer-sbm.com, or visit www.springeronline.com. Apress Media, LLC is a California LLC and the sole member (owner) is Springer Science + Business Media Finance Inc (SSBM Finance Inc). SSBM Finance Inc is a **Delaware** corporation.

For information on translations, please e-mail editorial@apress.com; for reprint, paperback, or audio rights, please email bookpermissions@springernature.com.

Apress titles may be purchased in bulk for academic, corporate, or promotional use. eBook versions and licenses are also available for most titles. For more information, reference our Print and eBook Bulk Sales web page at www.apress.com/bulk-sales.

Any source code or other supplementary material referenced by the author in this book is available to readers on GitHub via the book's product page, located at www.apress.com/9781484237441. For more detailed information, please visit www.apress.com/source-code.

Printed on acid-free paper

Table of Contents

About the Author

Ben Tyers is a freelance programmer and technical writer by day and a sci-fi horror novel writer by night. He made his first computer game way back in 1984 on a ZX Spectrum 48K computer when he was eight years old. His passion for creation has continued since then. He holds a number of computer-related qualifications. When relaxing, Ben has an infatuation for old-school horror and sci-fi films, particularly 1960s B movies.

About the Technical Reviewer

Dickson Law is a GameMaker hobbyist, commentator, and extension developer with six years of community experience. In his spare time, he enjoys writing general-purpose libraries, tools, and articles covering basic techniques for GameMaker Studio. As a web programmer, his main areas of interest include integration with server-side scripting and API design. He lives in Toronto, Canada.

Acknowledgments

Spot the Difference Backgrounds: Natalie Hubbert
Spot the Difference Clock: 123rf.com

Snake Beep Sound: Greencouch/FreeSound.org
Snake Double Beep Sound: InspectorJ Freesound.org
Snake GameOver Voice: (c) Ben Tyers/Monty Lewis Sauerwein
Snake Music: Eric Matyas/www.soundimage.org
Snake Sprites: nido/GraphicRiver.ent
Snake Background: antkevyv/123rf.com

Match Three Sweets: oglsdl/OpenGameArt.org
Match Three Star: Ecrivain/OpenGameArt.org

Dart Dartboard: VectorPortal.com
Dart Font: Darrell Flood
Dart Background: Prasong Takham/123rf.com
Dart Dart: pngtree.com
Dart Voices: (c) Ben Tyers/Monty Lewis Sauerwein
Dart Thud Sounds: Dane S Casperson/FreeSound.org

Quiz Images: Medals Julien/OpenGameArt.org

Rock, Paper, Scissors Images: Komain Techanadt/123rf.com
Rock, Paper, Scissors Audio: (c) Ben Tyers/Monty Lewis Sauerwein

Jet Pack Backgrounds: GameBuildingTools.com
Jet Pack Birds: Bevouliin.com/OpenGameArt.org
Jet Pack Player: Bevouliin.com/OpenGameArt.org
Jet Pack UFO: UFO Carlos Alface/OpenGameArt.org
Jet Pack Bullet: Napoleon/OpenGameArt.org
Jet Pack Explosion: J-Robot/OpenGameArt.org
Jet Pack Voices: (c) Ben Tyers/Monty Lewis Sauerwein
Jet Pack Music and Sound Effects: Eric Matyas/SoundImage.org

ACKNOWLEDGMENTS

Platform Game Ladder and Platforms: Kenney.nl
Platform Game Player Sprite: Spyros Kontis
Platform Game Audio: Eric Matyas/SoundImage.org

Bomber Player Sprites: Spyros Kontis
Bomber Sprites: Kenney.nl
Bomber Fruit: keith carnage/OpenGamrArt.org
Bomber Bomb Sprite: truezipp/OpenGameArt.org
Bomber Explosion: Ben Tyers
Bomber Game Audio: Eric Matyas/SoundImage.org

Tower Defense Towers and Missiles: Kenney.nl
Tower Defense Arrow: IgnasD/OpenGameArt.org
Tower Defense Smoke: KnoblePersona/OpenGameArt.org
Tower Defense Explosion: samoliver/OpenGameArt.org
Tower Defense Blood: PWL/OpenGameArt.org
Tower Defense Heart: cdgramos/OpenGameArt.org
Tower Defense Missile: Napoleon/OpenGameArt.org
Tower Defense Coin: galangpiliang/OpenGameArt.org

Introduction

Thank you for purchasing my book!

This book offers step-by-step instructions for making 10 mini games. Each chapter covers a different game.

The games have been chosen to introduce you to some of the features of the integrated development environment (IDE) and GameMaker Language (GML). It is strongly suggested that you create these games in the order that they are presented in this book. Each game assumes you have studied and understood the content and concepts of the previous chapter(s).

By the end of this book you will have a sound knowledge of the fundamentals of GameMaker Studio 2. You will have the skills needed to start making your own games and possibly the start of a career in the game-making industry.

Resources for this book can be accessed via the **Download Source Code** button located at www.apress.com/9784842374441.

CHAPTER 1

Spot the Difference

In this chapter, you will make a basic Spot the Difference game. The coding is quite simple, and it's a great way to start exploring the IDE. All of the images used in the game are available in the Resources folder that you downloaded. This project uses a background image and instances of an object to mark where the differences are, plus a control object for keeping track of the player's progress.

The aim of this game is for the player to find all of the differences between two images before time runs out.

When you start GMS2, you will be presented with the start screen shown in Figure 1-1.

© Ben Tyers 2018
B. Tyers, *Practical GameMaker Projects*, https://doi.org/10.1007/978-1-4842-3745-8_1

Figure 1-1. *The Start screen*

Click New, as shown in Figure 1-1, and then select GameMaker Language, as shown in Figure 1-2.

Figure 1-2. *Starting a GameMaker Language project*

Next, give the project a name, for example **spot**, as shown in Figure 1-3.

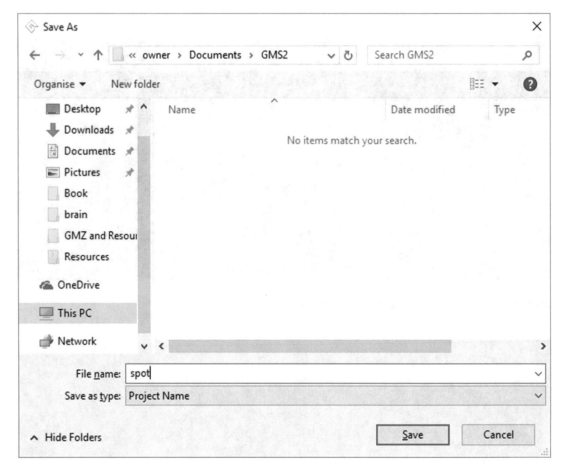

Figure 1-3. *Setting a name for a project*

You will be presented with a screen like the one shown in Figure 1-4.

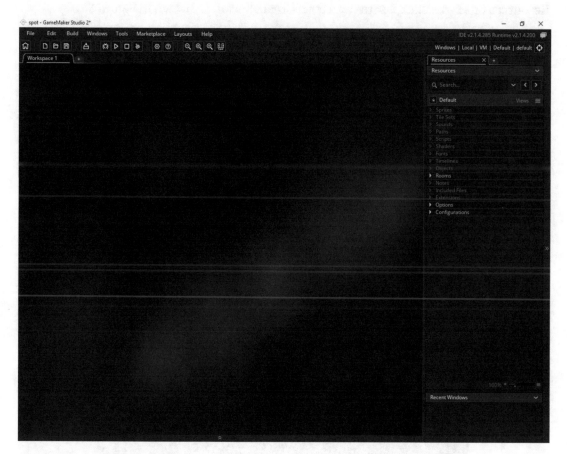

Figure 1-4. *The initial start screen*

This may look a little daunting at first, but don't worry; after you have completed the first five chapters of this book, you will be comfortable enough to find your way around this screen. If the Resources tab is not shown on the right of the window, you can click Windows in the top menu and then Resources.

This game of Spot the Difference uses four images, so load them now. In the Resources tab, right-click Sprites and then Create Sprite, as shown in Figure 1-5.

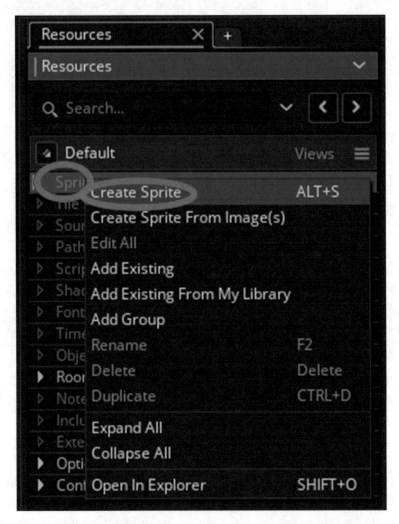

Figure 1-5. *Creating a new sprite*

Next, name the sprite **bg_1** and click Import, as shown in Figure 1-6.

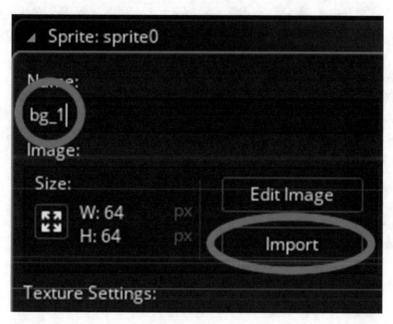

Figure 1-6. *Naming the sprite and importing it*

Navigate to the Resources folder and load in **Spot_Level_1**, as shown in Figure 1-7.

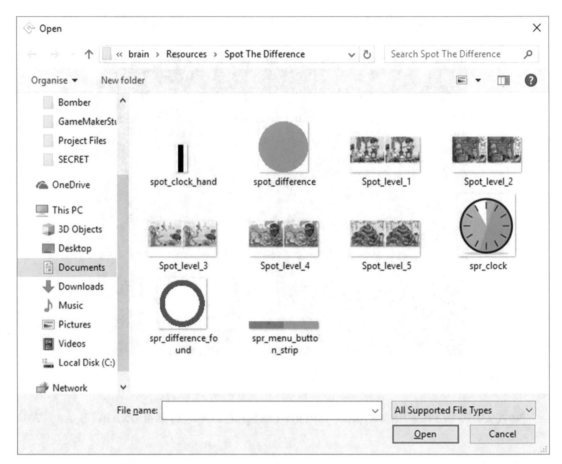

Figure 1-7. *Loading in a sprite*

When the dialog pops up, click Yes, as shown in Figure 1-8. You can also check the "Don't show the message again" box, also shown in Figure 1-8.

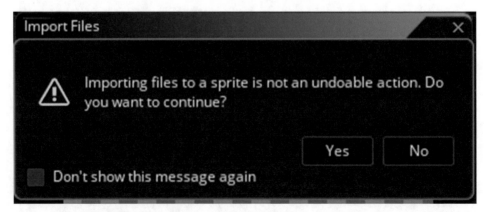

Figure 1-8. *Dialog pop-up*

Your screen will look something like Figure 1-9.

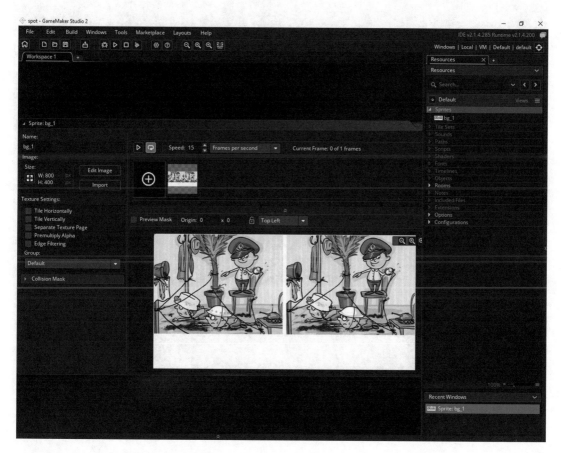

Figure 1-9. *A sprite loaded in*

Now, save and close this window. There are a few ways to do this. The first is to drag the window title with the left mouse button held down and then click the X. The second is to hold down the middle mouse button in an empty area and drag the workspace contents so you can see the close X box, as shown in Figure 1-10, and click it.

Figure 1-10. *One method of closing a window*

You can also right-click the window bar and select Close, as shown in Figure 1-11.

Figure 1-11. *The other method of closing a window*

Now, create a new sprite named **bg_2** and load in another resource so it looks like Figure 1-12.

Figure 1-12. *The bg_2 setup*

Next, create a sprite named **spr_menu_button** and load it in. This sprite is a little different. Set the name of the sprite and click Edit Image, as shown in Figure 1-13.

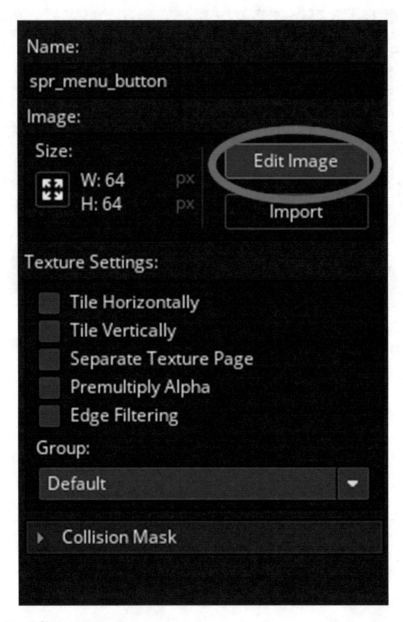

Figure 1-13. *Editing an image*

Click Image ➤ Import Strip Image. Select **spr_menu_button_strip**, as shown in Figure 1-14.

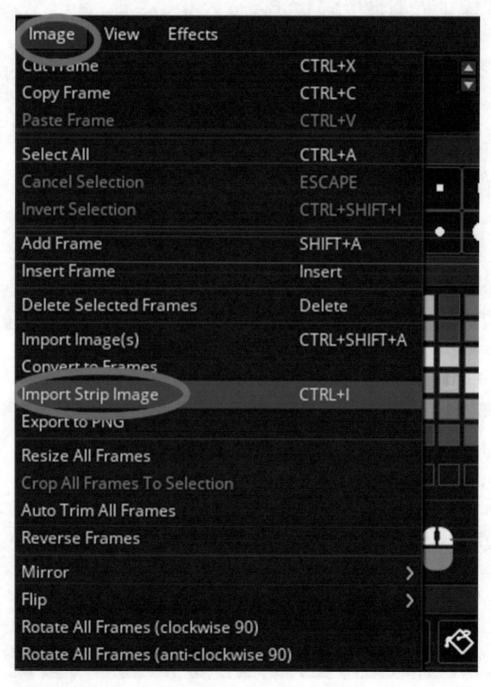

Figure 1-14. *Importing a strip image*

Set the number of frames and frames per row to 2, the frame width to 275, and the frame height to 55, as shown in Figure 1-15.

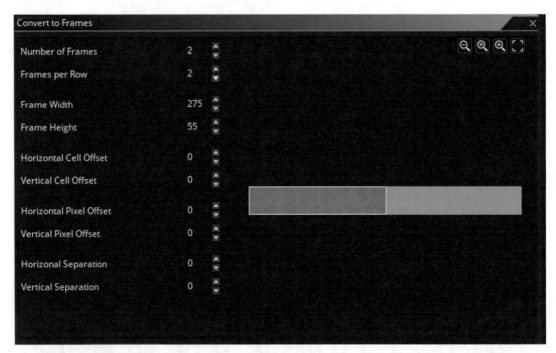

Figure 1-15. *Settings for the sprite strip*

Next, click Convert. You can close this window by clicking the X shown in Figure 1-16.

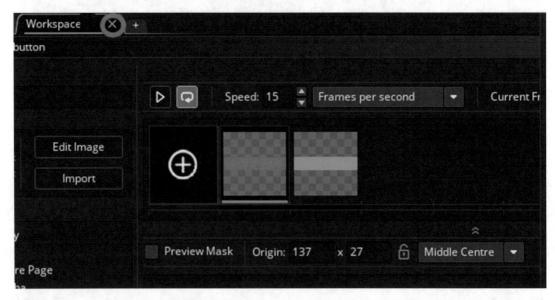

Figure 1-16. *Closing the sprite editor*

The final thing to set up for this sprite is the origin. The sprite origin is the place where the image is anchored when it is placed into a room. Set this as middle center, as shown in Figure 1-17.

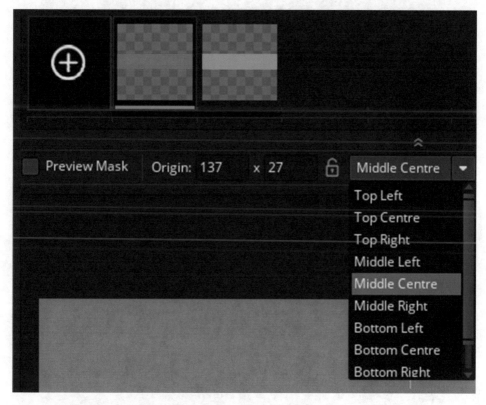

Figure 1-17. *Setting the sprite origin as middle center*

You can now close this window.

Next, create two sprites named **spr_face** and **spr_difference** and set the origin to middle center for both. The sprites needed for this are in the Resources folder. You should now be able to do this without screenshots.

Next, create a couple of fonts to use for drawing. You can create a new font by right-clicking Fonts in the Resources tree, as shown in Figure 1-18. Create two fonts. One is **font_info**, which is Arial size 12, and the other is **font_hud**, which is Arial size 19. These fonts can then be set to draw text in whatever font style and size you have set.

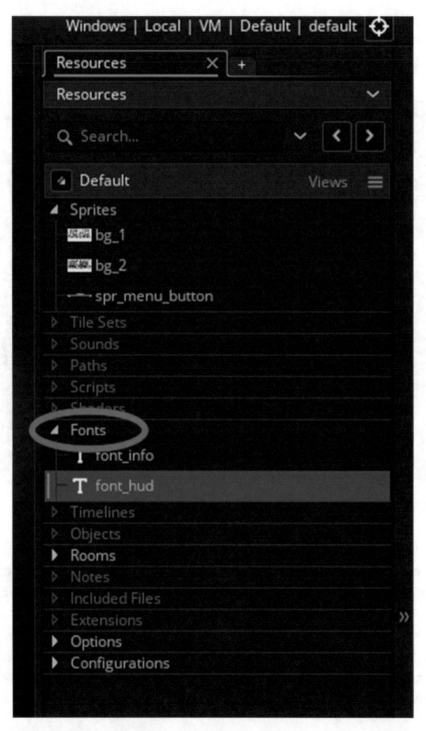

Figure 1-18. *Creating a new font*

In this game, you save the player's progress in something called an INI file. These files allow for easy saving and loading of data. This data is generally loaded at the start of the game. You will create an object to load any data.

First, you need to create an object. Right-click on Objects in the Resources tree and create a new object named **obj_splash**, as shown in Figure 1-19.

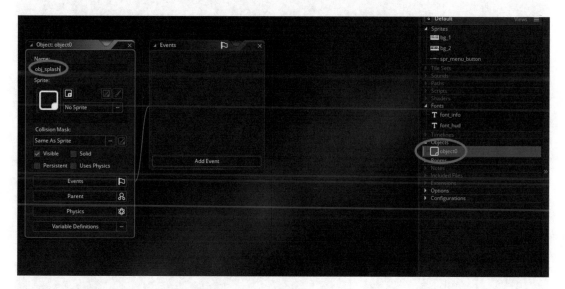

Figure 1-19. *Creating and naming an object*

Next, add some code to an event. Let's add this code to a **Create Event**. Click Events ➤ Add Events ➤ Create, as shown in Figure 1-20.

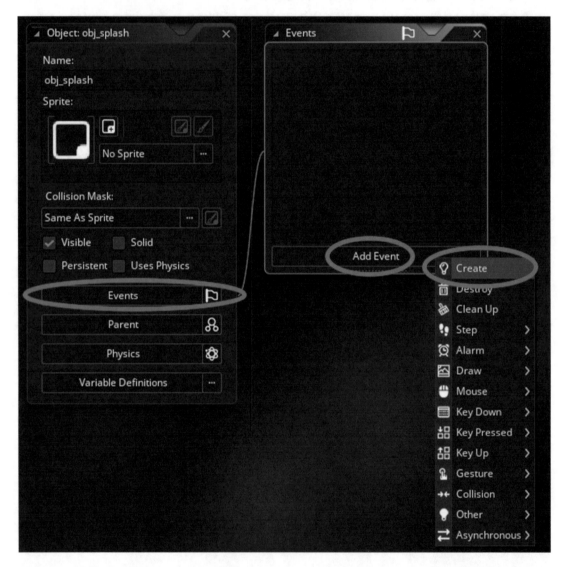

Figure 1-20. *Adding a Create Event*

Your screen will look something like Figure 1-21.

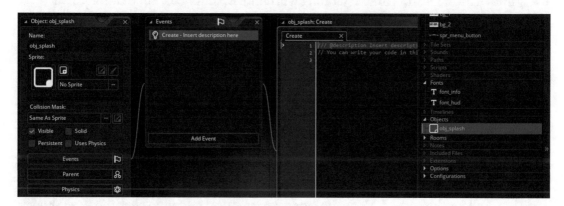

Figure 1-21. *An object with an event added*

It is possible at this stage that you will not be able to see the full window of the **Create Event**. By clicking in an empty area of the workspace, you can move it around to make it visible using middle mouse button, as shown in Figure 1-22.

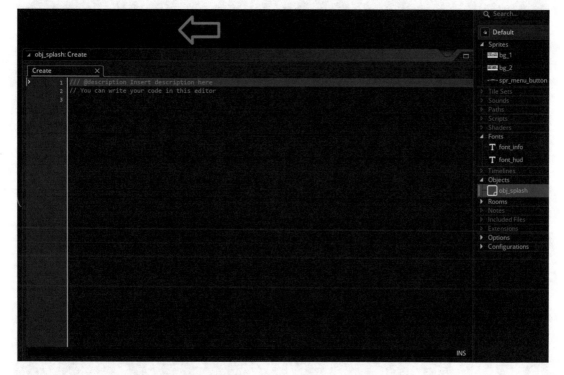

Figure 1-22. *Moving the workspace*

In the **Create Event**, type in the following code. Don't worry if you don't understand every line of the code; this understanding will come in time. This code starts with a comment and then opens **save.ini** (if it exists) and loads the level that the player picks or sets it as a default value of 1 if it is not present. It then goes to the room called **room_menu**. Note that the code almost reads like English, which makes it easy to understand.

```
/// @description Load Saved Level
ini_open("save.ini");
global.level = ini_read_real("save", "level", 1);
ini_close();
room_goto(room_menu);
```

That is all for this object. Move the workspace around and then click the X, as shown in Figure 1-23.

Figure 1-23. *Closing the object and applying changes*

Next, create two objects for the menu room. They are **obj_level_1_button** and **obj_level_2_button**. Make the objects clickable so the player can choose which room (level) to go to.

Create a new object by right-clicking Objects in the Resources tree. Name this object **obj_level_1_button** and assign it the sprite **spr_menu_button**, as shown in Figure 1-24.

Figure 1-24. *Assigning a sprite to an object*

Next, create a **Create Event** and add the following code, which will set the sprite's image index to 0 (green, showing it is unlocked and playable) or 1 (red and not unlocked):

```
/// @description Set Up Button
image_speed=0;
my_id=1;
if global.level>=my_id
{
    image_index=0;
}
else
{
    image_index=1;
}
```

Next, make a **Draw Event** by clicking Add Event ➤ Draw ➤ Draw, as shown in Figure 1-25.

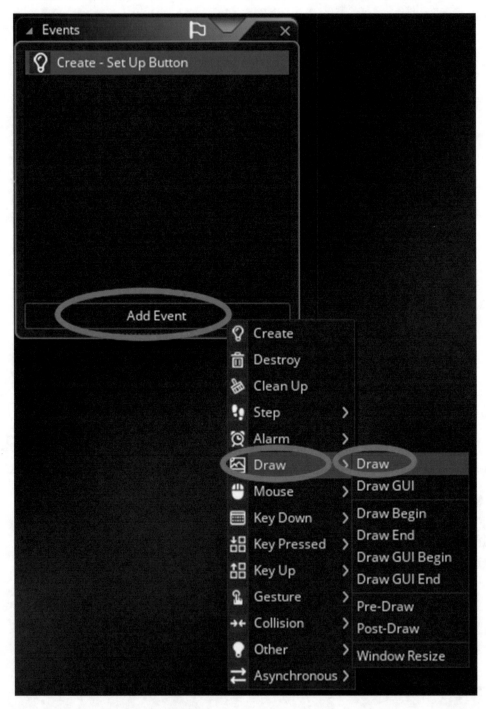

Figure 1-25. *Making a Draw Event*

Add the code for the **Draw Event**. It draws itself (the image index that has been set), sets the font and drawing color, sets the horizontal alignment to center, and then draws the text depending whether it is unlocked or locked:

```
/// @description Draw Button & Info
draw_self();
draw_set_font(font_info);
draw_set_colour(c_white);
draw_set_halign(fa_center);
if global.level>=my_id
{
    draw_text(x,y,"Level"+string(my_id)+"Unlocked");
}
else
{
    draw_text(x,y,"Level"+string(my_id)+"Locked");
}
```

Next, create the **Mouse Left Button Pressed Event**. This can be found at Add Event ➤ Mouse ➤ Left Pressed, as shown in Figure 1-26.

23

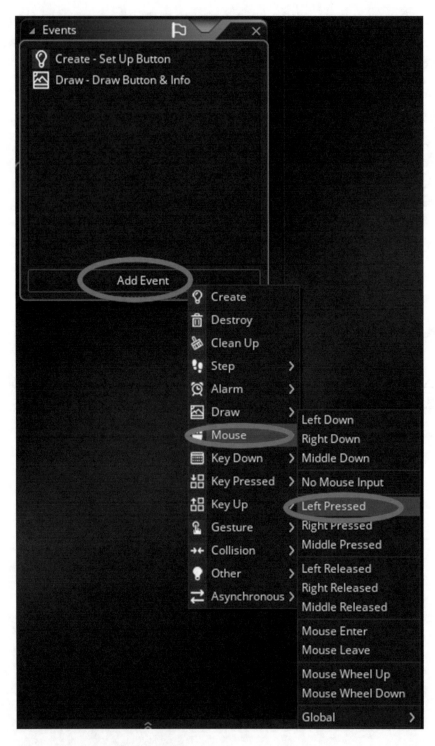

Figure 1-26. *A Mouse Left Pressed Event*

The GML for this event takes the player to room **room_level_1** if it is unlocked, which it will be:

```
/// @description Check If Unlocked
if global.level>=my_id
{
    global.this_level=my_id;
    room_goto(room_level_1);
}
```

That is all for this object. The next object is **obj_level_2_button**. Assign the same sprite to it as before. The **Create Event** code is similar to the previous object, except **my_id** is set to 2:

```
/// @description Set Up Button
image_speed=0;
my_id=2;
if global.level>=my_id
{
    image_index=0;
}
else
{
    image_index=1;
}
```

Add the **Draw Event** code. It is the same as the **Draw Event** GML for **obj_level_1_button**.

```
/// @description Draw Button & Info
draw_self();
draw_set_font(font_info);
draw_set_colour(c_white);
draw_set_halign(fa_center);
if global.level>=my_id
{
    draw_text(x,y,"Level"+string(my_id)+"Unlocked");
}
else
```

```
{
    draw_text(x,y,"Level "+string(my_id)+" Locked");
}
```

Add the **Left Mouse Pressed Event** code. It will only take the player to room **room_level_2** if the player has successfully completed the first level:

```
/// @description Check If Unlocked
if global.level>=my_id
{
    global.this_level=my_id;
    room_goto(room_level_2);
}
```

That is all for this object. You can now close it.

The next object is **obj_gameover**. There is no sprite for this object. Add a **Create Event** with code to start an alarm, which is a timer that counts down and triggers an **Alarm Event**. This code sets the alarm to 5 seconds:

```
/// @description set alarm
alarm[0]=room_speed*5;
```

Next, add an **Alarm 0 Event**, which can be accessed by Add Event ➤ Alarm ➤ Alarm 0, as shown in Figure 1-27.

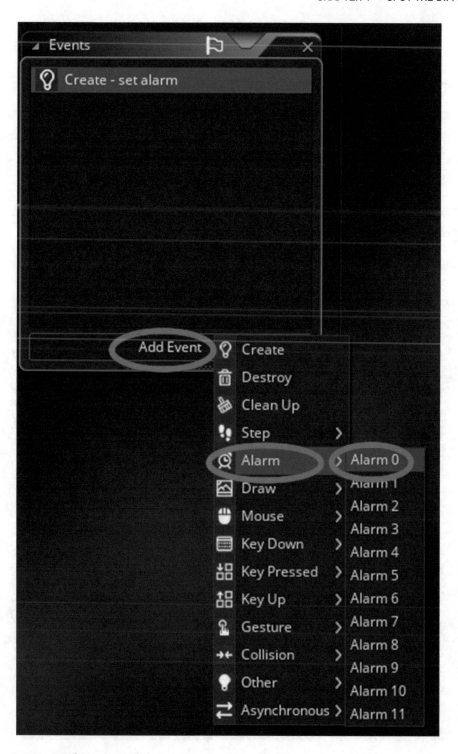

Figure 1-27. *Making an Alarm 0 Event*

The code for this **Alarm 0 Event** restarts the game when it triggers:

```
/// @description Restart game
game_restart();
```

Now add a **Draw Event** with the following code. This code draws the text "Game Over" on the screen. Note that you are not setting the font, alignment, or color. The settings for drawing text from the previous settings still apply. If you want to change the font, alignment, or color, do so before drawing the text.

```
/// @description Draw GameOver
draw_text(400,200,"Game Over");
```

When set up, it will look like Figure 1-28.

Figure 1-28. *The obj_gameover setup*

The next object is **obj_clockhand**, which makes use of two sprites. Create a new sprite named **spr_clock** and load in the sprite **spr_clock**. This time you want the origin set at the middle of the clock face. This origin is used to place the clock's hand in the correct place. Set the origin to 36 and Custom, as shown in Figure 1-29.

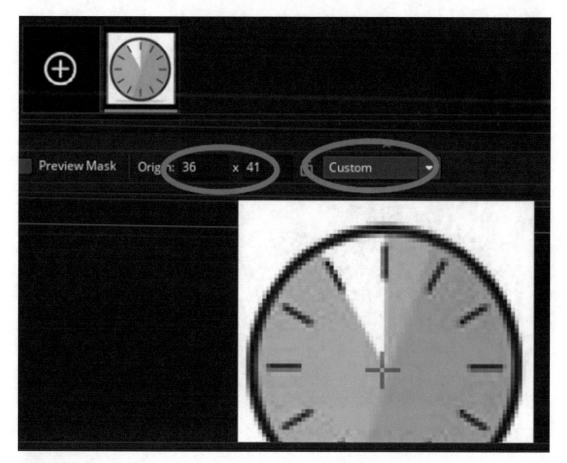

Figure 1-29. *Setting the sprite origin in the middle of the clock face*

You can now close this sprite by clicking the X at the top right of the window or right-clicking the title bar and selecting Close.

Next is the sprite for the hand. It uses a sprite named **spr_clockhand**. Make it now and set the origin as 6x31 and Custom, as shown in Figure 1-30.

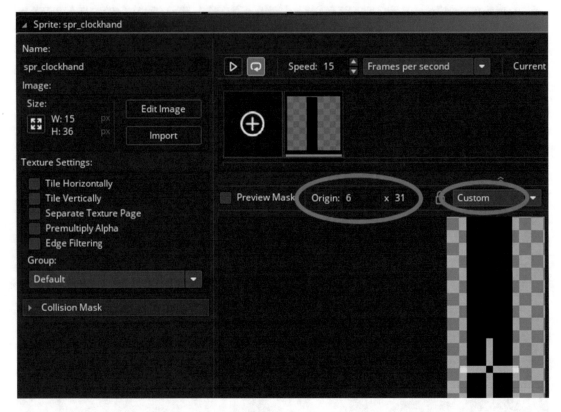

Figure 1-30. *Setting up spr_clockhand*

Open the object named **obj_clockhand** and enter the following **Create Event** code. This code sets the time to a starting value of 360 and starts an alarm with a time of one second:

```
/// @description Set Up
time=360;
alarm[0]=room_speed;
```

Next, make a **Step Event** by clicking Add Event ➤ Step ➤ Step, as shown in Figure 1-31.

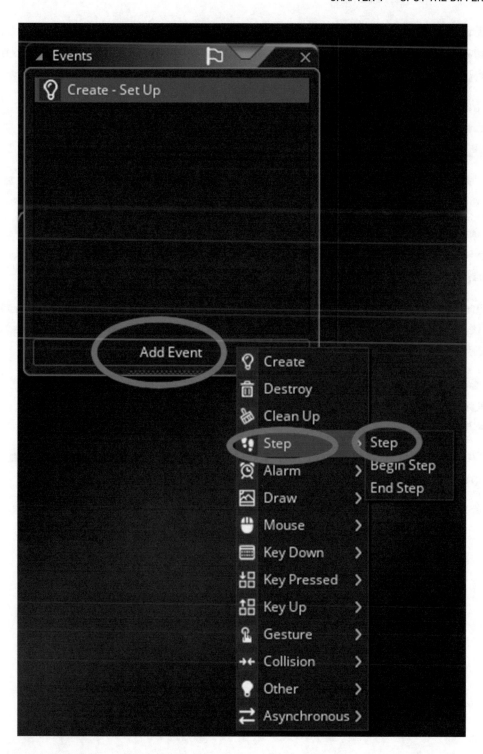

Figure 1-31. *Adding a Step Event*

The code for this **Step Event** tests the value of time. If it is equal to 0, it means that the player has run out of time and the game is over, so the player is taken to the room **room_gameover**:

```
/// @description check time & Set hand angle
if time==0 room_goto(room_gameover);
image_angle=time;
```

Next, make an **Alarm[0] Event** and add the following code, which reduces the value of time by 1 and then sets the alarm for 1 second again:

```
/// @description Set Time & Alarm
time--;
alarm[0]=room_speed;
```

And finally add a **Draw Event** with the following code, which draws the clock face and the hand at the angle of the value of time, making the hand slowly move around as the value of time changes:

```
/// @description Draw Face & Hand
draw_sprite(clock_face,0,x,y);
draw_self();
```

The next object is **obj_difference_found** with the sprite **spr_difference_found** set up as 32 x 32, as show in Figure 1-32, and the origin set as middle center.

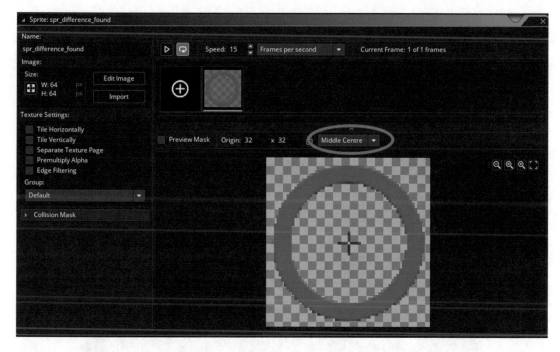

Figure 1-32. *The sprite set up with origin as middle center*

That is all for this object.

The next object is **obj_difference** and it has the sprite **spr_difference** with its origin as center. Go ahead and make this sprite now.

Set this object so that it is not visible to the player when the game is played. This can be done by unchecking the box shown in Figure 1-33.

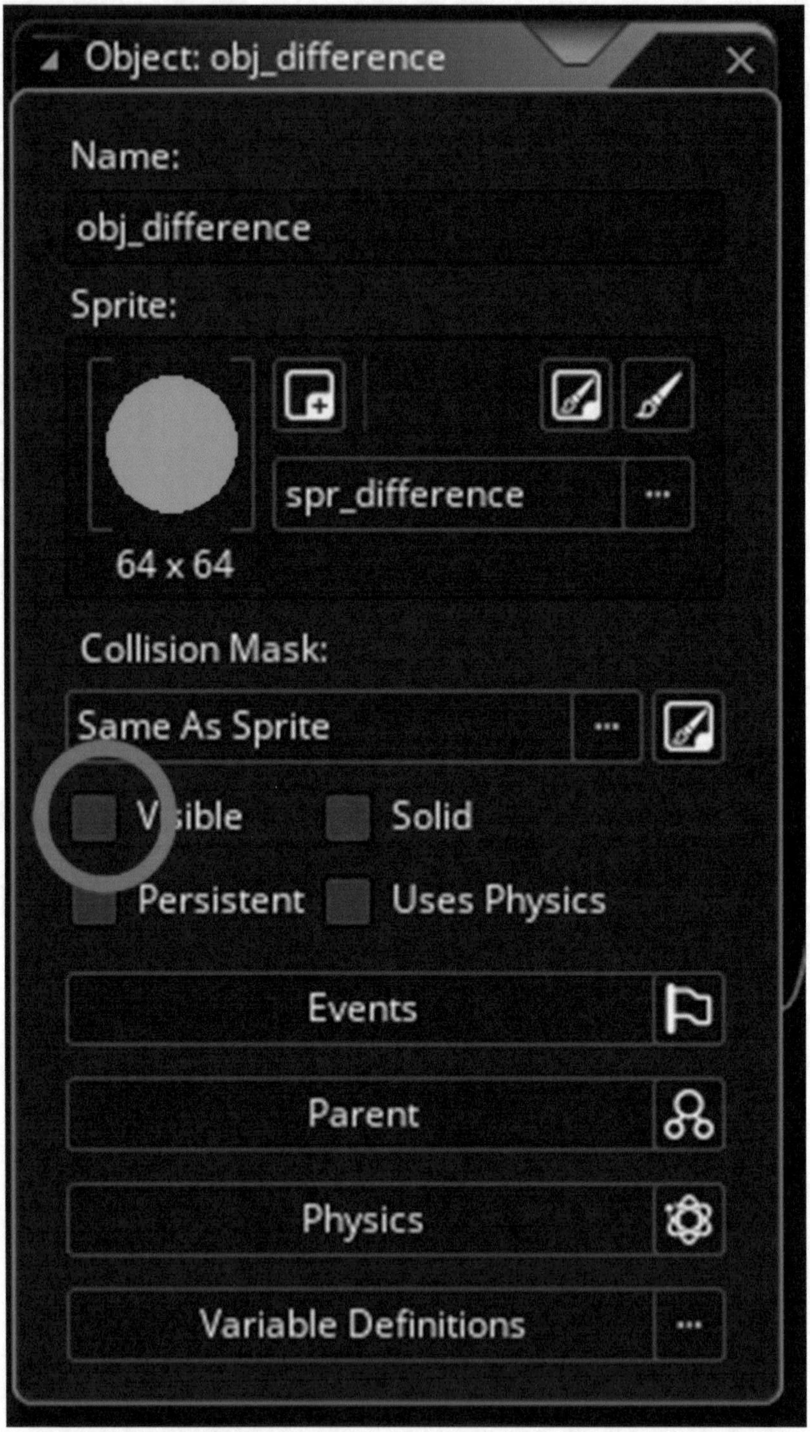

Figure 1-33. *Visible is unchecked*

This object has a **Left Mouse Button Pressed Event** with code that creates an instance of object **obj_difference_found** if the player clicks where the instance is placed:

```
/// @description Insert description here
instance_create_layer(x,y,"Instances",obj_difference_found);
instance_destroy();
```

This is shown in Figure 1-34.

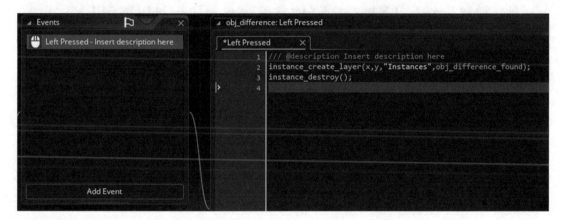

Figure 1-34. *The code for the Left Mouse Button Pressed Event*

The final object is **obj_hud**. There is no sprite for this object. Add a **Create Event** that sets the initial value of how many guesses the player has left:

```
/// @description Setup
guesses_left=15;
```

Next, add a **Step Event** with GML that checks whether the player has found all of the differences. If they haven't, they go to **room_gameover**; if they have, it saves the player's progress and they go back to **room_menu**:

```
/// @description guesses correct / out of moves
guesses_correct=instance_number(obj_difference_found);
if !instance_exists(obj_difference)
{
    if global.this_level==global.level
    {
        global.level++;
```

```
        ini_open("save.ini");
        ini_write_real("save", "level", global.level);
        ini_close();
    }
    room_goto(room_menu);
}
if guesses_left==0 room_goto(room_gameover);
```

Next, add a **Draw GUI Event** by clicking Add Event ➤ Draw ➤ Draw GUI, as shown in Figure 1-35.

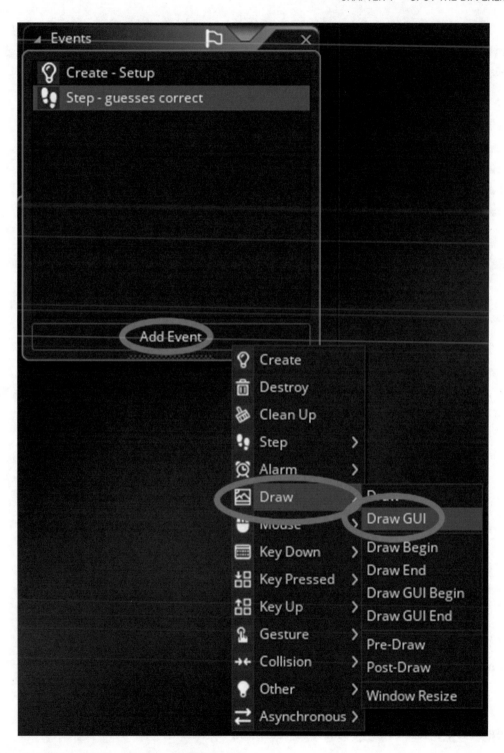

Figure 1-35. *Adding a Draw GUI Event*

Use the following code for this **Draw GUI Event**. It draws text above the standard **Draw Event** and is independent of any view. It sets the font, alignment, and color, and draws the guesses left and how many differences the player has found:

```
/// @description Draw HUD Info
draw_set_font(font_hud);
draw_set_halign(fa_left);
draw_set_colour(c_blue);
draw_text(40,360,"Guesses Left"+string(guesses_left));
draw_text(240,360,"Found"+string(guesses_correct));
```

Finally, add a **Global Left Pressed Event** with code to reduce the value of **guesses_left** by 1:

```
/// @description Draw HUD Info
guesses_left--;
```

That is all the code.

Next, you need to set up some rooms where the game will take place.

You can create a new room by right-clicking Rooms in the Resources tree. Right-click four times to create four new rooms, so it looks like Figure 1-36.

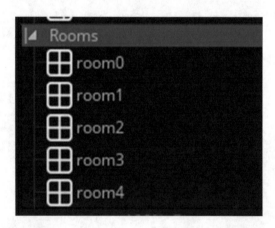

Figure 1-36. *Four new rooms*

Now right-click and rename the rooms as **room_splash**, **room_menu**, **room_level_1**, **room_level_2**, and **room_gameover**, as shown in Figure 1-37.

Tip The room order is important because the room at the top is the room that will run when the game starts.

Figure 1-37. *The room order*

Now let's make things happen.

First, you should tidy up the workspace. Create a new workspace by clicking the plus sign shown in Figure 1-38.

Figure 1-38. *Creating a new workspace*

Then right-click Workspace 2 ➤ Close All But This, as shown in Figure 1-39.

Figure 1-39. *One method of tidying up the workspace*

Now set up the rooms. Drag room **room_splash** as shown in Figure 1-40.

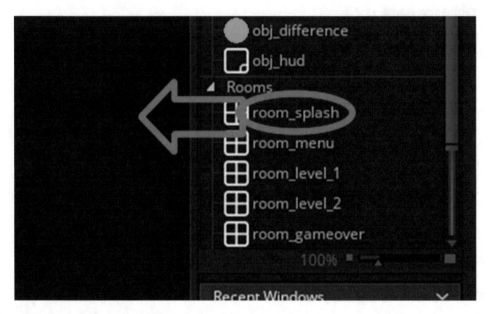

Figure 1-40. *Dragging a room to open it up*

Tip   Sometimes when opening a room, not all of the tabs are shown. You can click Reset Windows on Current Desktop to make them visible again.

First, set the dimensions of the room. Click Room ➤ Room Properties, as shown in Figure 1-41.

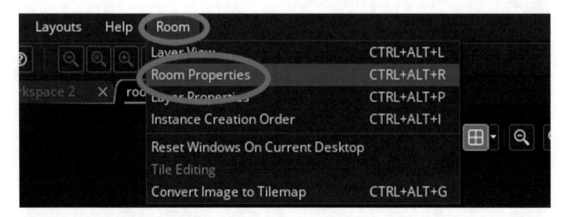

Figure 1-41. *Opening the room properties*

Set the height to 400 and width to 800, as shown in Figure 1-42.

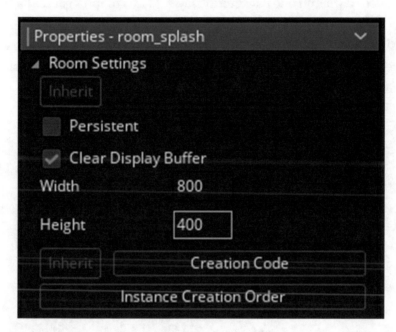

Figure 1-42. *Setting the room's dimensions*

Now click Room ➤ Layer View. Then click Instances in the Layers section, as shown in Figure 1-43.

Figure 1-43. *Setting a room layer*

Layers are used to determine the order in which instances are drawn. This game uses just one instances layer and one background layer. More complex games have multiple layers.

Now add an object to this room. This can be done by simply dragging an object from the Resources tree and placing it in the room. Go ahead and drag **obj_splash** into this room, as indicated in Figure 1-44.

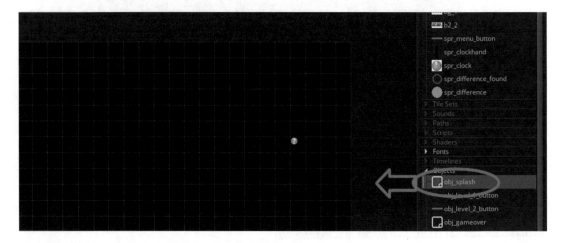

Figure 1-44. *One method of adding an object to a room*

That is all for this room. It can be closed now.

The next room is **room_menu**. Set it to size 800 x 400 and add one instance each of **obj_level_1_button** and **obj_level_2_button**, as shown in Figure 1-45, making sure the Instances layer is selected.

Figure 1-45. *Instances placed in room on the Instances layer*

That is all for this room. Close any open boxes.

Next, open up **room_gameover**, set the size to 800 x 400, and place one instance of **obj_gameover** in it on the Instances layer, as shown in Figure 1-46.

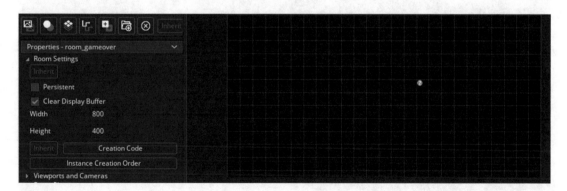

Figure 1-46. *room_gamover with its size set and an instance of obj_gameover placed*

That is all for this room.

Next, open up **room_level_1** and set the dimensions to 800 x 400. Next, select Background from the Layers tab. From the Resources tree, drag **bg_1** across, as shown in Figure 1-47.

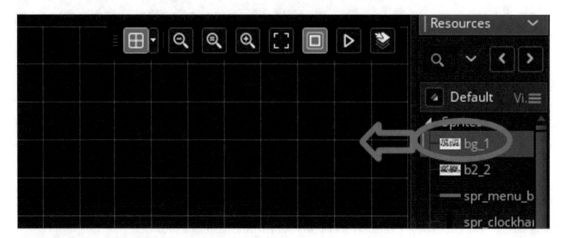

Figure 1-47. *Adding a background*

When placed, it will look like Figure 1-48.

Figure 1-48. *A room with the background set*

Next, select the Instances layer, as shown in Figure 1-49.

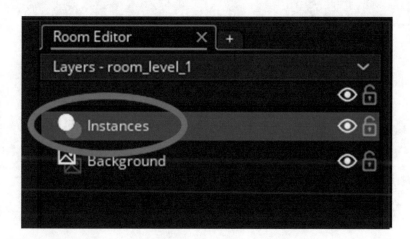

Figure 1-49. *Selecting the Instances layer*

Next, add one instance each of **obj_clockhand** and **obj_hud**, as shown in Figure 1-50.

Figure 1-50. *Instances placed in a room*

Next, place 10 instances of **obj_difference** in the places where the differences are. Click **obj_difference** in the Resources tree to highlight it. If you hold down the Alt key, you can place these instances with the left mouse button. The differences are shown in Figure 1-51.

Figure 1-51. *Placing the difference objects*

That is all for this room.

Repeat the process for **room_level_2**, using sprite **bg_2**.

Now is a great time to save and test the game. Click File in the top left and select Save.

To play the game, press F5 or click the Play arrow shown in Figure 1-52.

Figure 1-52. *Click the Play arrow to play the game*

Your game should look like Figure 1-53.

Figure 1-53. *The game in progress*

A project file for the completed game is in the Resources folder, which includes an extra level setup and some images for you to use to make your own levels.

EXTRA IDEAS FOR YOU TO TRY

1. Create a cool graphical effect when the player finds a difference.

2. Display a message if the player finds all of the differences in less than 30 seconds.

3. Export the game so it can be played on another computer.

4. Make the differences fade to 0.5 alpha once created.

5. There are additional Spot the Difference images in the Resources folder. Use them to make extra levels.

CHAPTER 2

Quiz

In this chapter, you'll create a multiple choice quiz. It's intended as an introduction to data and file handling. You do not need to understand every single line of the code; just try to understand the concepts being taught. This game will allow questions to be loaded from code or downloaded from a website as a text file and imported into the game, with the player aiming to get as many correct answers as possible.

So, start GameMaker Studio 2, start a new GML project, and name it something like Quiz.

If you completed Chapter 1 successfully, you should now know how to create and name sprites and load images in. You can also create a new sprite by right-clicking in an empty area of the workspace and selecting the resource that you wish to create.

Load in from the Resources folder and name the following sprites:

- **spr_button** with an origin of middle center
- **spr_clock** with an origin at the middle of the clock's face
- **spr_clock_hand** with an origin at position 6x4
- **spr_from_code** with an origin of middle center
- **spr_from_web** with an origin of middle center
- **spr_question_bg** with an origin of middle center

The sprite named **spr_badge** is a strip consisting of three frames. Create it and click Edit ➤ Image ➤ Import From Strip Image. Set the number of frames and frames per row to 3, frame width to 249, and frame height to 209, as shown in Figure 2-1.

© Ben Tyers 2018
B. Tyers, *Practical GameMaker Projects*, https://doi.org/10.1007/978-1-4842-3745-8_2

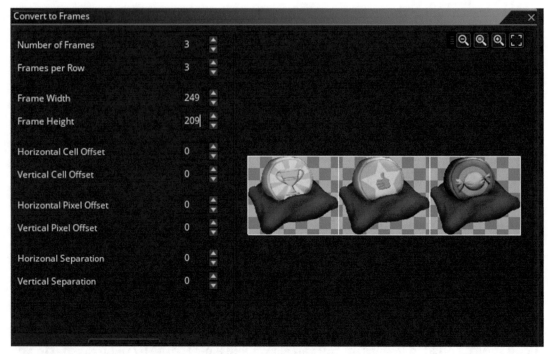

Figure 2-1. *Import settings for the sprite strip*

The first object is **obj_add_from_code**, which has no sprite. Add the following code to the **Create Event**. It sets up some initial game values and data structures known as arrays, which hold the question, answer options, and the correct answer:

```
/// @description Set For Data
global.current_question=1;
global.number_of_questions=5;
global.correct=0;

global.question[1]="What is the capital of England?";
global.option1[1]="London";
global.option2[1]="Paris";
global.option3[1]="New York";
global.answer[1]=1;

global.question[2]="What is a female swan called?";
global.option1[2]="Sow";
global.option2[2]="Pen";
global.option3[2]="Kitten";
global.answer[2]=2;
```

```
global.question[3]="How many legs does a dog have?";
global.option1[3]="1";
global.option2[3]="2";
global.option3[3]="4";
global.answer[3]=3;

global.question[4]="What is the square root of 16?";
global.option1[4]="2";
global.option2[4]="4";
global.option3[4]="8";
global.answer[4]=2;

global.question[5]="What colour is the moon?";
global.option1[5]="Blue";
global.option2[5]="Gray";
global.option3[5]="Purple";
global.answer[5]=2;

room_goto(room_quiz);
```

That is all for this object.

The next object is **obj_add_from_web**. It has no sprite. Add a **Create Event** with the following code. It downloads a file from a website that holds the questions, answer options, and correct answer in a text file. This is an asynchronous event, which basically means it works in the background while the game continues.

```
/// @description Get File 7 Set up
//Next line sets file to path and target
file = http_get_file("http://www.gamemakerbook.com/quiz.txt",working_
directory +"quiz.txt");
```

The next event is an **Async HTTP Event**, which can found by clicking Add Event ➤ Asynchronous ➤ Async - HTTP, as shown in Figure 2-2.

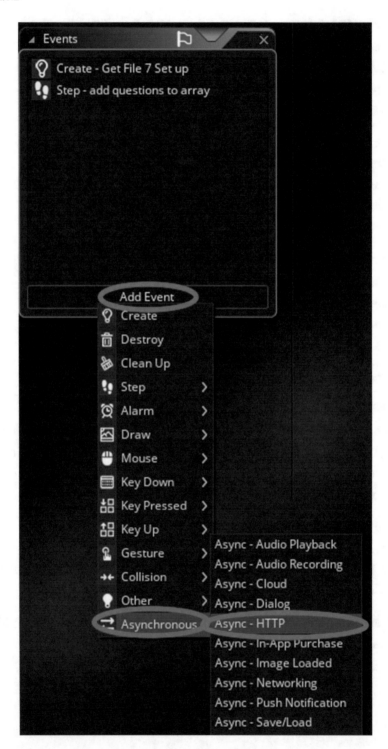

Figure 2-2. *Adding an asynchronous HTTP event*

The code for this event sets to true once the file has successfully downloaded:

```
/// @description async status check
if ds_map_find_value(async_load, "id") == file //sets up map
{
    var status = ds_map_find_value(async_load, "status"); //gets status
    if status == 0//status 0 means file is finished downloading
    {

        //openfile
        file=file_text_open_read(working_directory +"quiz.txt");
        while (!file_text_eof(file))//loops until end of file
        {
            num++;
            global.question[num]=file_text_read_string(file);
            file_text_readln(file);
            global.option1[num]=file_text_read_string(file);
            file_text_readln(file);
            global.option2[num]=file_text_read_string(file);
            file_text_readln(file);
            global.option3[num]=file_text_read_string(file);
            file_text_readln(file);
            global.answer[num]=file_text_read_real(file);
            file_text_readln(file);
        }
        file_text_close(file);//closes file
        //add questions to array
        global.current_question=1;
        global.number_of_questions=num;
        global.correct=0;
        room_goto(room_quiz);
    }
}
```

That is all for this object.

Next is **obj_ask**. Assign it sprite **spr_question_bg** and add a **Step Event** that checks if all questions have been asked:

```
/// @description if no more questions
if global.current_question>global.number_of_questions
{
    room_goto(room_result);
}
```

Next, add a **Draw Event** that formats text for drawing and then draws the player's current progress through the questions:

```
/// @description draw info & question
draw_self();
draw_set_font(font_info);
draw_set_halign(fa_center);
///Info and questions
draw_text(x,y+10,"Number of Questions"+string(global.number_of_questions));
draw_text(x,y+30,"Current Question"+string(global.current_question));
draw_text(x,y+50,global.question[global.current_question]);
```

That is all for this object.

Next up is **obj_timer**. Assign it **spr_clockface**. Add a **Create Event** that sets a value for holding how much time the player has remaining and sets an alarm to reduce it every second:

```
/// @description set time and start alarm
global.time=30;
alarm[0]=room_speed;
```

Next, add a **Step Event** that keeps the time at a maximum value of 60 and checks if the player has run out of time. If the player has run out of time, they are sent to the result room.

```
/// @description Check time
if global.time>60 global.time=60;
if global.time==0
```

```
{
    room_goto(room_result);
}
```

Next, add an **Alarm 0 Event** with GML that reduces the value of **time** and resets the alarm to 1 second. Note that **global.time--;** reduces the value by 1; it is the same as using **global.time=global.time-1**; or **global.time-=1;**.

```
/// @description reduce time and set alarm again
global.time--;
alarm[0]=room_speed;
```

And finally add a **Draw Event** that draws the clock face, the hand, and some text, showing the player how much time they have remaining:

```
/// @description draw clock and face
draw_self();
//draw hand
var hand_angle=180-(global.time*6);
draw_sprite_ext(spr_clock_hand,0,x,y,1,1,hand_angle,c_white,1);

//draw seconds as text
draw_set_font(font_info);
draw_set_halign(fa_center);
draw_set_colour(c_red);
draw_text(x,y+75,string(global.time)+"Seconds");
```

That's all for this object.

The next three objects are the buttons that the player presses to select an answer. The first object is **obj_option_1**. Assign it **spr_button**. Add a **Draw Event** that draws the button for the question and the appropriate answer for that option:

```
/// @description draw button and answer option
draw_self();
draw_set_font(font_info);
draw_set_halign(fa_middle);
draw_set_colour(c_black);
draw_text(x,y,global.option1[global.current_question]);
```

Next, add a **Left Pressed Mouse Button Event** that checks the array to see if the player has chosen the correct answer option. It shows a message based on whether the answer was correct and awards a point if so. It then increases the value of the current question so the next question can be asked.

```
/// @description check if correct
if global.answer[global.current_question]==1
{
    show_message("correct");
    global.correct++;
    global.current_question++;
    global.time+=10;
}
else
{
    global.current_question++;
    show_message("not correct");
}
```

That is all for this object. The next two buttons are **obj_option_2** and **obj_option_3**. They are very similar. In fact, just one line of code needs to be changed, so you can use the duplicate function to create these objects. In the Resources tree, right-click **obj_option_1** and then Duplicate. Do this twice. This is shown in Figure 2-3.

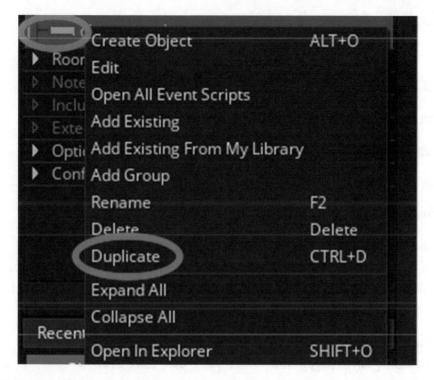

Figure 2-3. *Duplicating an object*

Rename one of these new objects as **obj_option_2**. Now make the changes to the code. In the **Left Pressed Event**, change

```
if global.answer[global.current_question]==1
```

to

```
if global.answer[global.current_question]==2
```

And in the **Draw Event**, change

```
draw_text(x,y,global.option1[global.current_question]);
```

to

```
draw_text(x,y,global.option2[global.current_question]);
```

That is all for this object.
Do the same for **obj_option_3** and change

```
if global.answer[global.current_question]==1
```

to

```
if global.answer[global.current_question]==3
```

And in the **Draw Event**, change

```
draw_text(x,y,global.option1[global.current_question]);
```

to

```
draw_text(x,y,global.option3[global.current_question]);
```

That is all for this object.

The next object is **obj_from_code**. Assign it **spr_from_code**. Add a **Mouse Left Button Pressed Event** that creates an instance of the object that sets the questions and answers from code, and destroys the two options:

```
/// @description Create Object To Load From Code
instance_create_layer(x,y,"instances",obj_add_from_code);
with (obj_from_code) instance_destroy();
with (obj_from_web) instance_destroy();
```

That is all for this object. The next object is **obj_from_web**. Assign it **spr_from_web**. Add a **Mouse Left Button Pressed Event** that creates an instance of the object that downloads the question file from the web and destroys the options:

```
/// @description Create Object to Load From Web
instance_create_layer(x,y,"Instances",obj_add_from_web);
with (obj_from_code) instance_destroy();
with (obj_from_web) instance_destroy();
```

That is all for this object.

The last object for this game is **obj_result**. Assign it **spr_infobg**. Add a **Draw Event** that displays the player's overall score and draws a badge depending on how many questions the player answered correctly (gold for 100% correct, silver for 50% or more, and bronze for under 50%):

```
/// @description Draw Result
if global.correct==global.number_of_questions
```

```
{
    badge="Gold"; //all correct
    draw_sprite(spr_badge,0,500,100);

}
else if global.correct>(global.number_of_questions/2)
{
    badge="Silver"; //over half
    draw_sprite(spr_badge,1,500,100);
}
else
{
    badge="Bronze"; //otherwise
    draw_sprite(spr_badge,2,500,100);
}

draw_self();
//draw text
draw_set_font(font_info);
draw_set_halign(fa_middle);
draw_set_colour(c_black);
draw_text(x-50,y,"You got"+ string(global.correct) +"Out of
"+string(global.number_of_questions));
draw_text(x-50,y+25,"Your badge is"+badge);
draw_text(x-50,y+75,"Press R to restart");
```

Next, add a **Key Pressed R Event**, which can be selected by clicking Add Event ➤ Key Pressed ➤ Letters ➤ R, as shown in Figure 2-4.

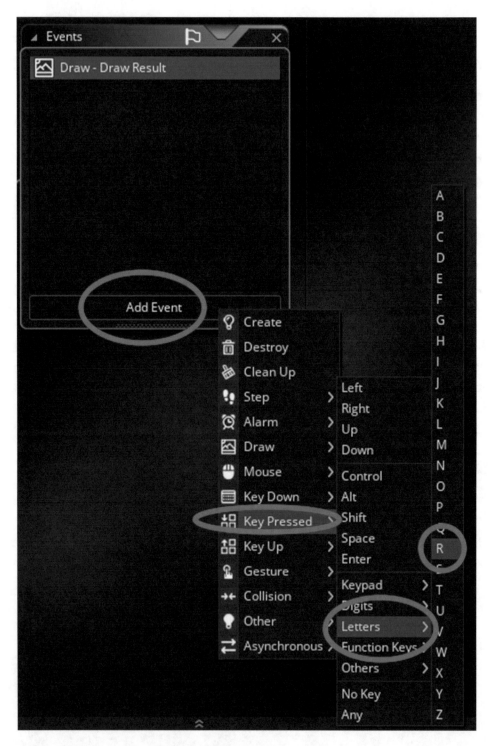

Figure 2-4. *Setting an event for the keypress of r*

The code for this keypress event restarts the game:

```
/// @description Restart
game_restart();
```

That is all the objects.

This game has three rooms. The first is **room_setup_quiz**. So create this room and drag it into a new workspace. If the necessary tabs are not showing, they can be selected from Room at the top of the screen, as shown in Figure 2-5.

Figure 2-5. *The options under Room*

Set the room size to 800 x 600. Select the Background layer and set it as white, as shown in Figure 2-6.

Figure 2-6. *Settting the background to white*

Next, select the Instances layer and add one each of **obj_from_code** and **obj_from_web**, as shown in Figure 2-7.

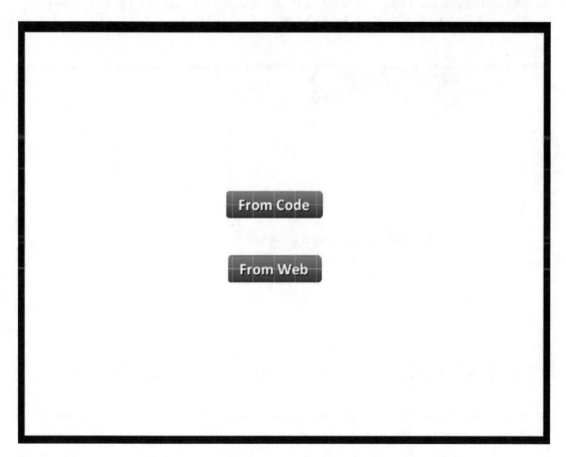

Figure 2-7. *room_setup_quiz with a white background and instances*

That is all for this room.

The next room is **room_quiz**. It is 800 x 600 in size and has the same background as the previous room. It has one instance of **obj_timer**, **obj_ask**, **obj_option_1**, **obj_option_2**, and **obj_option_3**, as shown in Figure 2-8.

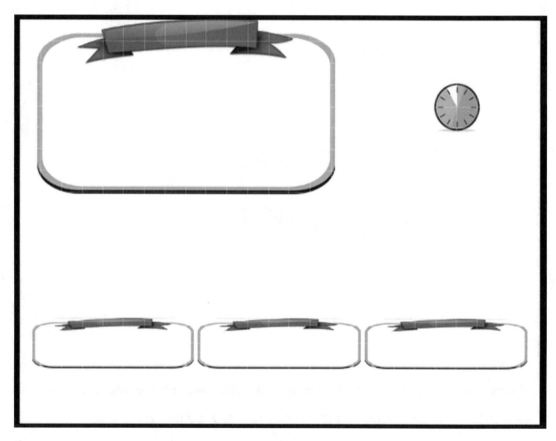

Figure 2-8. *room_quiz with instances placed*

That is all for this room.

The final room is **room_result**, with the same background of white and size of 800 x 600. It has an instance of **obj_result**, as shown in Figure 2-9.

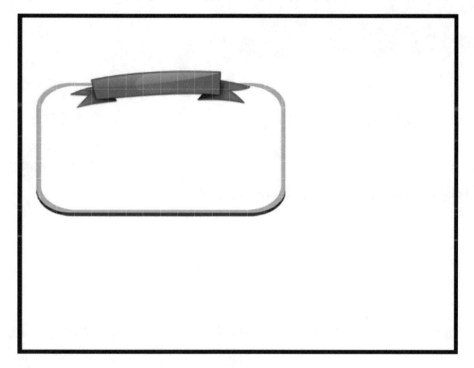

Figure 2-9.   *room_result with an instance of obj_result*

The final step is to create a font named **font_info**, which is Arial size 20. When you play the game, it will look like Figure 2-10.

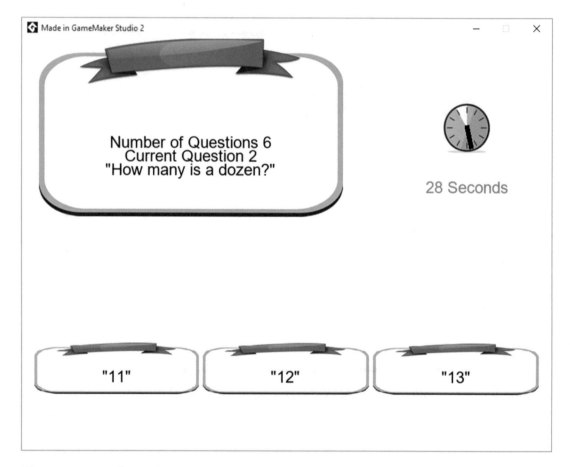

Figure 2-10. *The quiz game in action*

A project file for the completed game is in the Resources folder. Try making your own quiz as a text file and uploading it to a website.

EXTRA IDEAS FOR YOU TO TRY

1. Change the game so there are four answer options to choose from.

2. Make background music that changes when the player is running out of time.

3. At game start, give the player a choice of question topics and then load in an appropriate question file.

4. Create a program that allows a person to enter a question, possible answers, and the correct answer, which can be exported as a text file and then imported by this game.

5. Make a high score table that takes the player's name and how many correct answers they got.

CHAPTER 3

Snake

In this chapter, you will make a basic Snake game. Doing so will introduce you to using sounds and music as well as some important programming fundamentals such as enums and sprite manipulation. It will also build upon and reinforce what you learned in Chapters 1 and 2.

The aim of this game is to eat as much food as possible, without hitting the red blocks or any part of your tail.

Create a new GML project and name it Snake.

This game uses just five sprites. You can load them in now. The origin of all sprites is middle center. They are

- **spr_head**
- **spr_block**
- **spr_trial**
- **spr_food**
- **spr_bg**

This game also uses four sounds, one for background music and three sound effects. You can create a new sound by right-clicking Sounds in the Resources tree or by right-clicking in an empty area and selecting Resources ➤ Create Sound, as shown in Figure 3-1.

© Ben Tyers 2018
B. Tyers, *Practical GameMaker Projects*, https://doi.org/10.1007/978-1-4842-3745-8_3

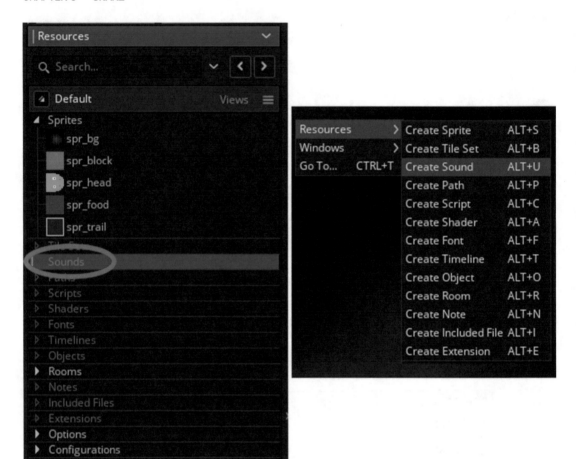

Figure 3-1. *Where to right-click to create a sound resource*

Name the new sound as **snd_music** and load the music from the Resources folder. When done, it will look like Figure 3-2.

Figure 3-2. *Sound resource added*

Repeat this process for **snd_food**, **snd_move**, and **snd_gameover**. When done, your Resources tree should look like Figure 3-3.

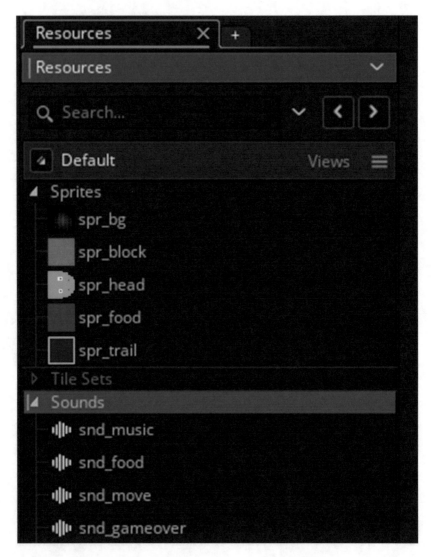

Figure 3-3. *The Resources tree*

Next, create a font named **fnt_score**, which is Arial size 20, as shown in Figure 3-4.

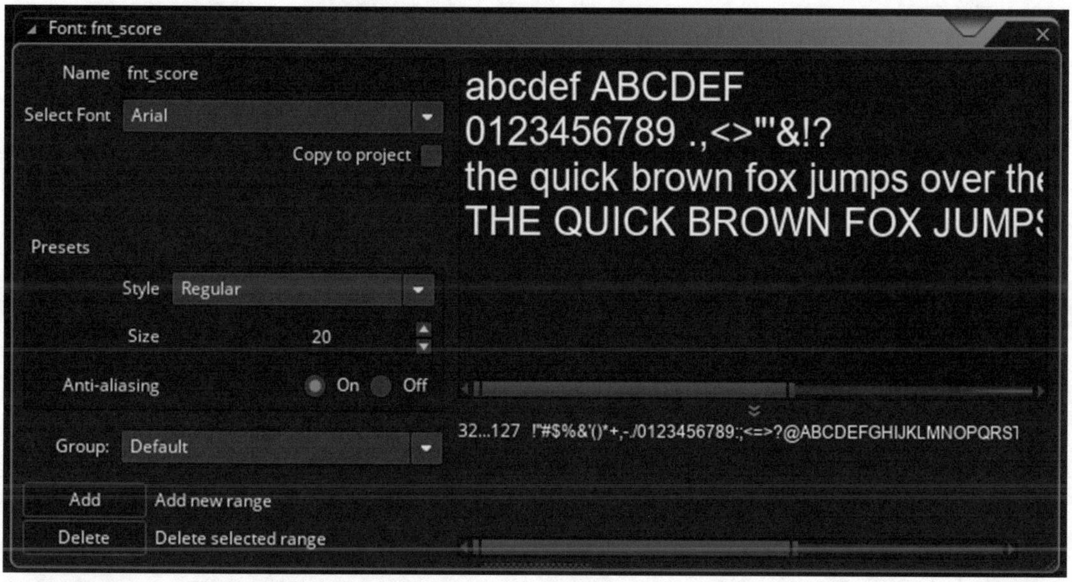

Figure 3-4. *Font settings*

The first object is **obj_startscreen**. There is no sprite for this object. Add a **Create Event** with code that opens the ini file called **highscore.ini** and loads any high score, if present; otherwise, it sets the high score to 0:

```
/// @description Load Highscore & Start Music
ini_open("highscore.ini");
global.highscore=ini_read_real("save","highscore",0);
ini_close();
audio_play_sound(snd_music,0,true);
```

Next, add a **Draw Event** with GML that draws the current high score and tells the player to press s to start the game:

```
/// @description Draw Highscore & info
draw_set_font(fnt_score);
draw_set_colour(c_green);
draw_set_halign(fa_center);
draw_text(320,320,"Highscore"+string(global.highscore));
draw_text(320,400,"Press S To Start Game");
```

Finally, add a **Key Press S Event** with code that takes the player to **room_game** upon a key being pressed:

```
/// @description Go to game room
room_goto(room_game);
```

That is all for this object.

The next object is **obj_food**. Assign the **spr_food** image to it. There is no code for this object.

Next up is **obj_block**. Assign sprite **spr_block** to it. Again, there is no code for this object.

Next is **obj_trail**. Assign **spr_trail** to it. This is the tail of the snake. Add a **Create Event** with code that sets an alarm based on the length of the snake:

```
/// @description Set Alarm
alarm[0]=global.length;
```

Next, add an **Alarm 0 Event** with GML that destroys the instance when alarm 0 triggers:

```
/// @description destroy on alarm
instance_destroy();
```

The next object is **obj_head**. Assign the **spr_head** sprite to it. Add a **Create Event** that sets up an enum and any initial values that the snake needs. An enum is a type of data that allows different states to be applied to it, in the direction that the snake can travel in.

```
enum state
{
    idle,
    up,
    down,
    left,
    right
}
dir=state.right;
move_size=16;
global.length=5;
alarm[0]=1;
room_speed=4;
```

Next, add a **Step Event**. Since there is only one statement after the conditional, I omitted the use of { and }; you can write the code with these brackets if you wish. The code for this event states the value of **dir** to one of the enum states you created, based on the key presses the player makes. It then plays a beeping sound and moves the snake's head to a new position.

```
/// @description Movement
//Keyboard
if keyboard_check_pressed(vk_left) dir=state.left;
if keyboard_check_pressed(vk_right) dir=state.right;
if keyboard_check_pressed(vk_up) dir=state.up;
if keyboard_check_pressed(vk_down) dir=state.down;

audio_play_sound(snd_move,1,false);
///movement
if dir==state.left//if moving left
{
    x-=move_size;//move
    image_angle=180;
}
if dir==state.right
{
    x+=move_size;
    image_angle=0;
}
if dir==state.up
{
    y-=move_size;
    image_angle=90;
}
if dir==state.down
{
    y+=move_size;
    image_angle=270;
}
```

Add an **Alarm 0 Event** that places an instance of **obj_trail** at the snake's position:

```
/// @description Create trail on alarm
instance_create_layer(x,y,"game",obj_trail);
alarm[0]=1;
score++;
```

The next event is called a **Collision Event**. This event is triggered when two instances (actually their bounding boxes) collide. You can make things happen when this event triggers. For this game, you want a **Collision Event** with **obj_food**. This is shown in Figure 3-5.

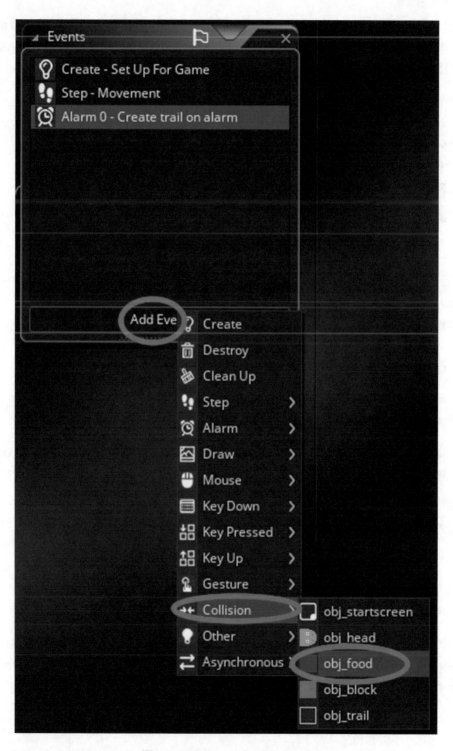

Figure 3-5. *Setting up a Collision Event with obj_food*

The code for this **Collision Event** with **obj_food** increases the length value of the snake, destroys the food, awards points, and creates a new instance in an empty position within the room but at least 32 pixels away from any border:

```
/// @description on collision
global.length+=1;
with (other) instance_destroy();
score+=250;
audio_play_sound(snd_food,1,false);

with (obj_trail) alarm[0]+=1;


do
{
    var xx=irandom_range(32,room_width-32;
    var yy= irandom_range(32,room_height-32;
}
until (place_free(xx, yy))//find a free place

food=instance_create_layer(xx,yy,"game",obj_food);
with(food) move_snap(16,16);
```

Next, add a **Collision Event** with **obj_trail**. It has the following code (which should not require any explanation):

```
/// @description Go to gameover room
room_goto(room_gameover);
```

Add another **Collision Event** with **obj_block** with the following code:

```
/// @description Go to gameover room
room_goto(room_gameover);
```

Next, add an **Outside Room Event**, which can be found by clicking Add Event ➤ Other ➤ Outside Room, as shown in Figure 3-6. Add the same code you used for Collision Event with obj_block.

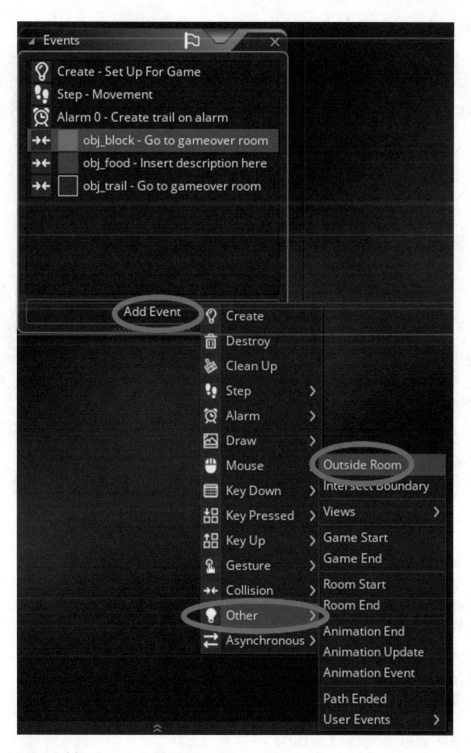

Figure 3-6. *Adding an Outside Room Event*

When done, the Events window will look like Figure 3-7.

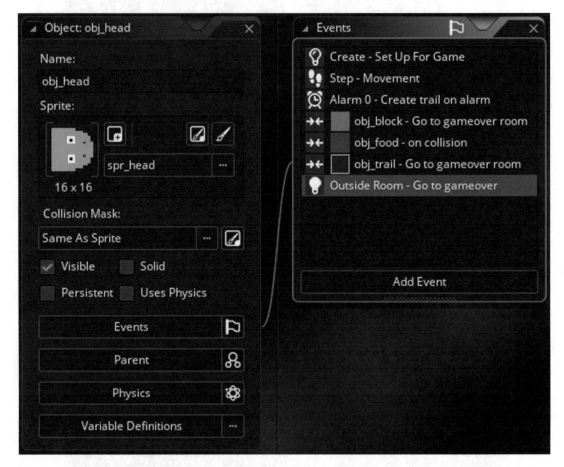

Figure 3-7. *The events for obj_head*

That is all for this object.

The next object is **obj_gameover**. Add a **Create Event** that stops the music, plays some audio, and updates the saved high score if the new score is greater than the previous high score:

```
/// @description Set Alarm - Stop Music & Save Score
alarm[0]=room_speed*10;
if audio_is_playing(snd_music)
{
    audio_stop_sound(snd_music);
}
```

```
audio_play_sound(snd_gameover,1,false);

if score>global.highscore
{
    ini_open("highscore.ini");
    ini_write_real("save","highscore",score);
    ini_close();
}
```

Add an **Alarm 0 Event** with the following code:

```
/// @description Restart Game
game_restart();
```

Add a **Draw Event** with the following code:

```
/// @description Draw Final Score
draw_set_font(fnt_score);
draw_set_halign(fa_center);
draw_set_colour(c_green);
draw_text(room_width/2,room_height/2,"Final Score" + string(score));
```

That is all for this object.

The final object is **obj_hud**, which has no sprite. The **Draw GUI Event** code draws the score and the high score at the top of the window, above any other instances:

```
/// @description Draw Score
draw_set_font(fnt_score);
draw_set_colour(c_green);
draw_set_halign(fa_center)
draw_text(160,40,"Score" + string(score));
draw_text(360,40,"Highscore" + string(global.highscore));
```

That is all for this object.

This game has three rooms.

Room **room_start_game** has one instance of **obj_startscreen** placed in it, as shown in Figure 3-8.

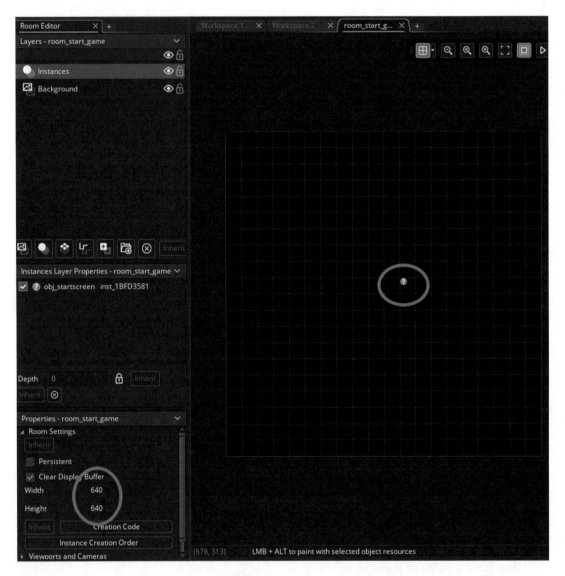

Figure 3-8. *room_start_game with an instance of obj_startscreen placed*

If your window is getting a little busy, feel free to close any open workspaces.

Create a new workspace, and drag over room **room_game**.

You can add instance layers and rename the Instance layer to **game**, also shown in Figure 3-9.

Select the Background layer and draw over **spr_bg**. Set it to Stretch, as shown in Figure 3-9.

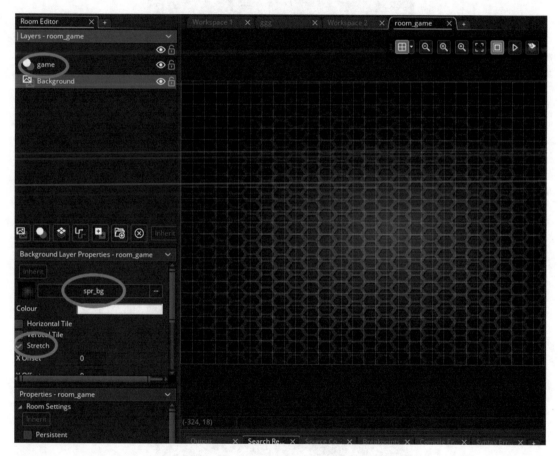

Figure 3-9. *Setting the background to stretch*

You will now set up a very large room. It's so large that you can only see one part of it at any time. This is called a view. You will set this view up to keep the player within this view. The settings for this are shown in Figure 3-10.

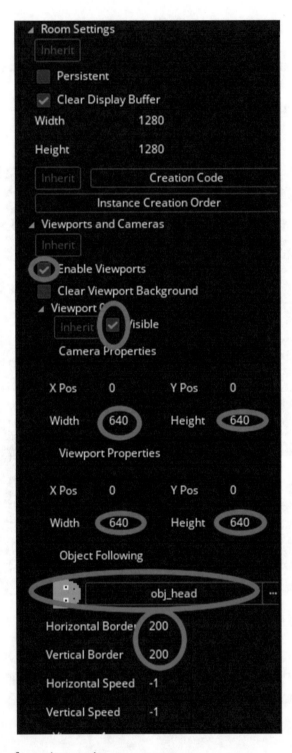

Figure 3-10. *Setup for using a view*

Next, select the game layer and place one instance of **obj_head**, one of **obj_hud**, and a few of **obj_food** and **obj_block**, as shown in Figure 3-11.

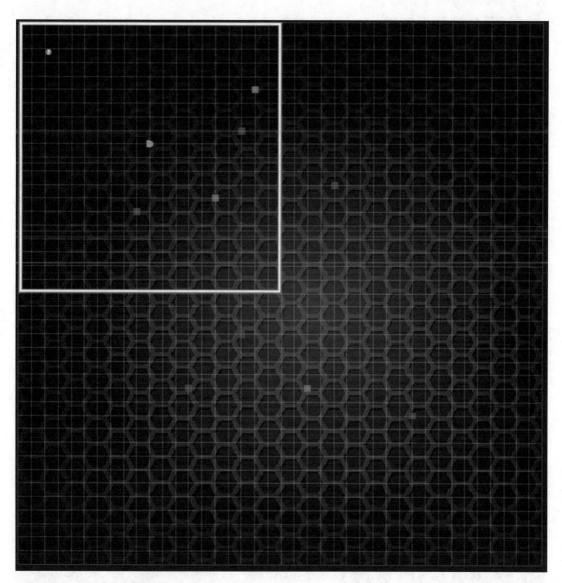

Figure 3-11. *Instances placed in room*

That is all for this room. You can now close it.

The final room is **room_gameover**, which is 640 x 740 in size and has an instance of **obj_gameover** placed in it.

Now is a good point to save and test your game.

Your game will look like Figure 3-12.

Figure 3-12. *The game in action*

A project file for the completed game is in the Resources folder.

EXTRA IDEAS FOR YOU TO TRY

1. Make a two-player version, with the aim of collecting 10 food items first.

2. Design a level with more objects to avoid.

3. Change the game so the player needs to eat food at least every 30 seconds. If they don't, they die.

4. Set it so the snake's tail starts with a length of 50.

5. Create a system that saves scores and displays the highest five scores on game start.

CHAPTER 4

Rock, Paper, Scissors

This chapter is a remake of the classic game of Rock, Paper, Scissors. This chapter will reinforce what you learned in the first three chapters and will introduce new concepts and coding.

This game has a very basic AI system that randomly allows the computer to choose either rock, paper, or scissors. The aim of this game is to outwit the computer by making a play that defeats it.

This game uses just three sprites:

- **spr_rock**
- **spr_paper**
- **spr_scissors**

Load them in now and set the origin of each to middle center.

This game uses four sounds:

- **snd_arr**
- **snd_ouch**
- **snd_prefect**
- **snd_yeah**

You can go ahead and load them in now.

This game makes use of something called a script. Basically, a script is a special block of code that can take in arguments (usually variables), perform an action, and return a result or not. Scripts are useful for a lot of reasons, but the most important use is to separate out complex code to make editing easier. They're also useful if you use similar code in more than one place.

You can create a script by right-clicking Script ➤ Create Script, as shown in Figure 4-1.

© Ben Tyers 2018
B. Tyers, *Practical GameMaker Projects*, https://doi.org/10.1007/978-1-4842-3745-8_4

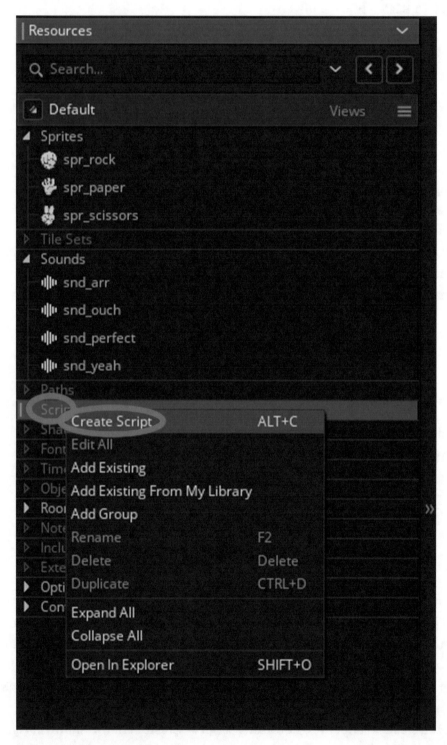

Figure 4-1. *Creating a script*

Right-click this in the Resources tree and rename it as **scr_play**, as shown in Figure 4-2. This script checks the player's and computer's play, returning a value of 0 for a draw, -1 for a loss, or 1 for a win. This code uses enumeration variables, which are defined elsewhere in this chapter. It tests a variable using a switch statement and finds the appropriate code section depending on its value. If you must check against multiple values, a switch statement is preferable; it's a tidier way of checking the values.

```
///scr_play(play1,play2)
switch (argument0) {
case play.rock:
    switch (argument1) {
        case play.paper: return -1;
        case play.scissors: return 1;
        default: return 0;
    }; break;
    case play.paper:
    switch (argument1) {
        case play.scissors: return -1;
        case play.rock: return 1;
        default: return 0;
    }; break;
    case play.scissors:
    switch (argument1) {
        case play.rock: return -1;
        case play.paper: return 1;
        default: return 0;
    }; break;
}
```

Figure 4-2. *The script set up with code*

Next, set up a font called **font_text** and set it as Arial size 25.

Create the first object, **obj_splash_and_setup**. No sprite is needed. Add a **Create Event** with code that sets up initial values and an enum. **randomize** is used to create a different selection of computer plays each time the game is run.

```
//set initial variables
global.player_wins=0;
global.computer_wins=0;
global.draws=0;
enum play
{
    none,
    rock,
    paper,
    scissors
}
global.computer_play=play.none;
global.player_play=play.none;
global.text="Player To Go - Click To Choose";
```

```
randomize();
```

```
room_goto(room_game);
```

That is all for this object.

The next object is **obj_player_play**, which has no sprite. Add a **Create Event** code that places the instances so the player can make their move:

```
///create buttons
instance_create_layer (200,400, "Instances",obj_button_rock);
instance_create_layer (400,400, "Instances",obj_button_paper);
instance_create_layer (600,400, "Instances",obj_button_scissors);
```

Add an **Alarm 0 Event** that removes the player's options and creates the instance needed for the computer to play:

```
///on alarm
instance_create_layer (x,y, "Instances",obj_computer_play);
with obj_button_rock instance_destroy();
with obj_button_paper instance_destroy();
with obj_button_scissors instance_destroy();
```

```
instance_destroy();
```

Next up is **obj_computer_play**. It has no sprite. Add **Create Event** code that makes the computer choose a number (1, 2 or 3) to make its move:

```
/// @description for Computer Hand
var play=irandom_range(1,3); //choose a random number
switch (play)
{
    case 1:
    {
        global.computer_play=play.rock;
        var hand="Rock";
        break;
    }
    case 2:
    {
```

```
        global.computer_play=play.paper;
        var hand="Paper";
        break;
    }
    case 3:
    {
        global.computer_play=play.scissors;
        var hand="Scissors";
        break;
    }
}
```

```
global.text="Computer Chooses"+hand;
alarm[0]=room_speed*2;
```

Next, add an **Alarm 0 Event** that creates the instance to display the result and then destroys itself:

```
///on alarm
instance_create(x,y, "Instances",obj_result);
instance_destroy();
```

The next object is **obj_global_drawing**; there is no sprite assigned to this object. Add a **Draw End Event**, which is shown in Figure 4-3.

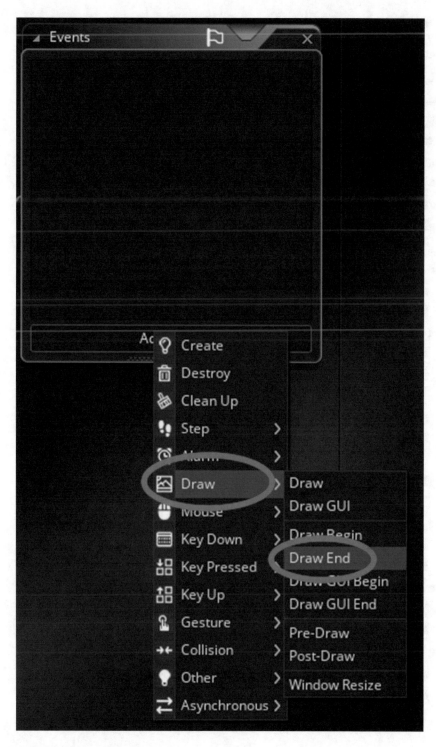

Figure 4-3. *The Draw End Event*

The code for this event draws the results of the current play:

```
/// @description draw game results
draw_set_font(font_text);
draw_set_halign(fa_center);
draw_set_colour(c_black);
draw_text(room_width/2,580,global.text);
draw_text(room_width/2,630,"Player Wins"+string(global.player_wins));
draw_text(room_width/2,680,"Computer Wins"+string(global.computer_wins));
draw_text(room_width/2,730,"Draws"+string(global.draws));
switch global.computer_play
{
    case play.rock:
        draw_sprite(spr_rock,0,room_width-200,200);
        break;
    case play.paper:
        draw_sprite(spr_paper,0,200,200);
        break;
    case play.scissors:
        draw_sprite(spr_scissors,0,room_width-200,200);
        break;
}
switch global.player_play
{
    case play.rock:
        draw_sprite(spr_rock,0,200,200);
        break;
    case play.paper:
    draw_sprite(spr_paper,0,200,200);
        break;
    case play.scissors:
        draw_sprite(spr_scissors,0,200,200);
        break;
}
```

The next object is **obj_result**, again with no sprite assigned. Add a **Create Event** with code that sets the text to display the result and then sets an alarm to 4 seconds:

```
/// @description do result
var result=scr_play(global.player_play, global.computer_play);

switch (result)
{
    case -1:
        global.computer_wins++;
        global.text="Computer Wins";
        audio_play_sound(choose(snd_arr,snd_ouch),1,false);
        break;
    case 0:
        global.draws++;
        global.text="Draw";
        audio_play_sound(choose(snd_arr,snd_ouch),1,false);
        break;
    case 1:
        global.player_wins++;
        global.text="Player Wins";
        audio_play_sound(choose(snd_perfect,snd_yeah),1,false);
        break;
}
alarm[0]=room_speed*4;
```

Next, add an **Alarm 0 Event** with code that resets the plays and restarts the room so the next round can be played:

```
///on alarm
global.computer_play=play.none;
global.player_play=play.none;
global.text="Player To Go - Click To Choose";
room_restart();
```

The next object is **obj_button_scissors**. Assign it **spr_scissors**. Add a **Mouse Left Released Event** with code that sets that the player has chosen scissors:

```
///on mouse click
global.player_play=play.scissors;
global.text="Player Chooses Scissors";
obj_player_play.alarm[0]=room_speed*2;
```

The next object is **obj_button_paper**. Assign it **spr_paper**. Add a **Left Mouse Released Event** with code that sets that the player has chosen paper:

```
//on mouse
global.player_play=play.paper;
global.text="Player Chooses Paper";
obj_player_play.alarm[0]=room_speed*2;
```

The final object is **obj_button_rock**. Assign it **spr_rock**. Add a **Left Mouse Released Event** with code that sets that the player has chosen rock:

```
///on mouse
global.player_play=play.rock;
global.text="Player Chooses Rock";
obj_player_play.alarm[0]=room_speed*2;
```

That's it. All of the objects are set up.

There are two rooms in this game. The first is **room_splash**; it is 800 x 768 in size and has one instance of **obj_splash_and_setup**.

The second room is **room_game**. Note that a background color of white is set. This room has one instance of **obj_global_drawing** and one of **obj_player_play**.

You can now save and test the game. It will look like Figure 4-4.

Figure 4-4. *The game in action*

A project file for the completed game is in the Resources folder.

EXTRA IDEAS FOR YOU TO TRY

1. Make it so two players can play against each other.

2. Make the computer play against itself 1,000 times and display the results.

3. Change the game to the variation known as Rock, Paper, Scissors, Lizard, Spock.

4. Create a save system that saves how many games the player has won, lost, and drawn.

5. Play an appropriate sound effect based on the outcome.

CHAPTER 5

Jet Pack

In this chapter, you will add to what you have learned so far to create a Jet Pack-style game with lots of features. This game will be made in multiple stages, meaning you can save and test the progress of the game as you make it.

The aim of this game is to shoot the enemies and destroy them.

So far in this book I have optimized the sprites so they are ready to import straight into the game. However, usually when you obtain graphics they won't be the format or the size you need for your game.

Go ahead and load in the main player's sprite.

Create a new sprite named **spr_player_1**. Import it and set it as shown in Figure 5-1.

© Ben Tyers 2018

B. Tyers, *Practical GameMaker Projects*, https://doi.org/10.1007/978-1-4842-3745-8_5

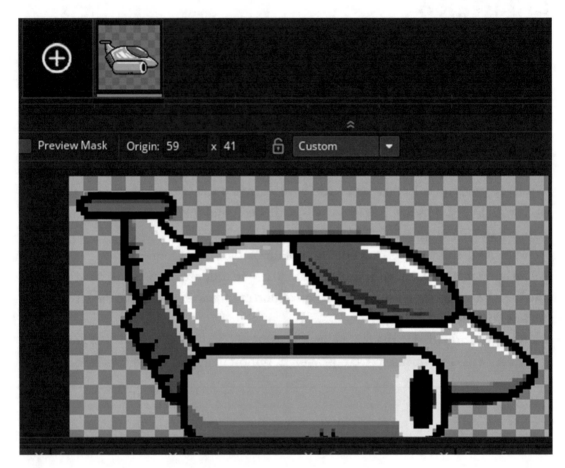

Figure 5-1. *The sprite's initial setting*

Next, create an object named **obj_player_1** and assign it the sprite you just created.

In a **Create Event**, enter the following code. This variable is used as the y position the player will return to if they are not moving up or down:

```
flying_level=200;
```

Next, create a **Key Down W Event**. It will trigger as long as the button is being held down. This event can be found by going to Add Event ➤ Key Down ➤ Letters ➤ W, as shown in Figure 5-2.

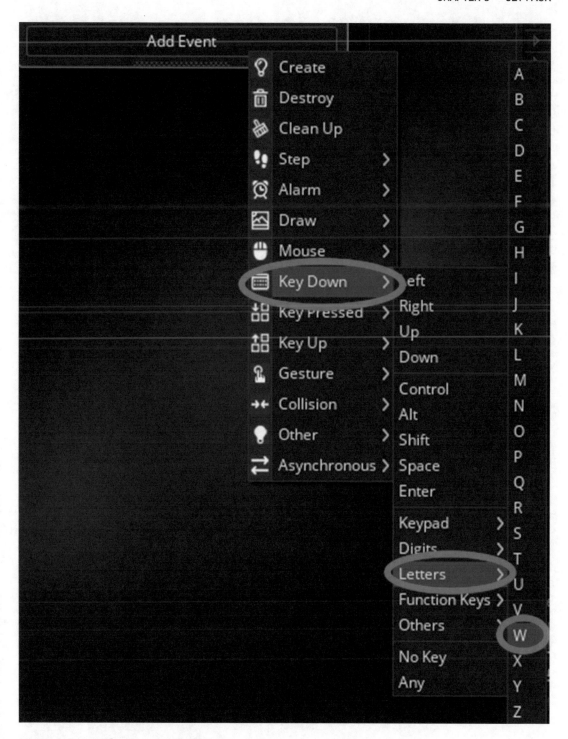

Figure 5-2. *The Key Down W Event*

Put the following code into this event. It moves the player up 5 pixels for every step that the key is held down:

```
/// @description move up
y-=5;
```

Next, make a **Key Down S Event** with code that moves the player down 5 pixels for each step the key is held down:

```
/// @description move down
y+=5;
```

Next, make a **Step Event** and add the following code. It sets a value for **global. difference** that is used for a parallax graphical effect. It also checks the value of y and prevents the player going off the top or bottom of the screen. The final two lines make the player slowly move back to the value of **flying_level**.

```
/// @description Object management
global.difference=(flying_level-y)/10; //set as a global value as it will
be used for parallax background
image_angle=global.difference-10;
//keep in screen
if y<20 y=20;
if y>380 y=380;
//prevent moving if key is being pressed
if !keyboard_check(ord("W")) or !keyboard_check(ord("S"))
{
    if y<flying_level y+=2;
    if y>flying_level y-=2;
}
```

Next, create a room called **room_game**, set the dimensions as 1000 x 600, and place in it one instance of **obj_player_1**. Now is a good point to save and test the game so far.

Next, add a feature known as parallax. It uses multiple backgrounds to create a sense of depth.

Load in sprites **bg_0**, **bg_1**, **bg_2**, and **bg_3**.

Open up a room and game and create three background layers, as shown in Figure 5-3. Ensure that the order of the backgrounds is the same as shown, so that the layers are drawn in the correct order.

Figure 5-3. *Background layers*

Set **bg_1** as the background image, check the Horizontal Tile box, and set the horizontal speed to -3, as shown in Figure 5-4.

Figure 5-4. bg_1 settings

Repeat the process for **bg_2**, setting the horizontal speed to -2.

Repeat the process for **bg_3**, setting the horizontal speed to -1.

Finally, create an object named **obj_road** and set the sprite **bg_0**. Select the Instances layer and add one of this object.

In order to have the player drawn above anything else, select the Instances layer and click the **obj_player_1** in the room and delete it by pressing Delete.

Now create a new instance layer and name it Player, so the order is as shown in Figure 5-5.

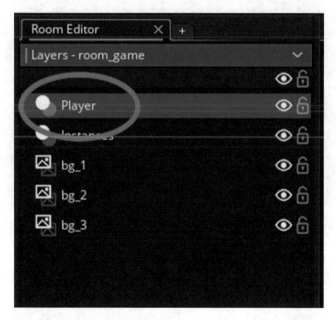

Figure 5-5. *Layers in order*

Add one instance of **obj_player_1** on this layer. Your room will look like Figure 5-6.

Figure 5-6. *The room all set up*

Now you want to make the backgrounds move up or down depending on the player's y position on the screen.

Open up **obj_player_1** and add the following code to the **Step Event**. It changes the y position of the backgrounds based on the value of **global.difference**, creating a parallax effect. Change the values to get different amounts of the parallax effect.

```
layer_y(bg_1,100+global.difference*2);
layer_y(bg_2,30+global.difference*1);
layer_y(bg_3,40+global.difference*0.5);
```

It should look like Figure 5-7 when done.

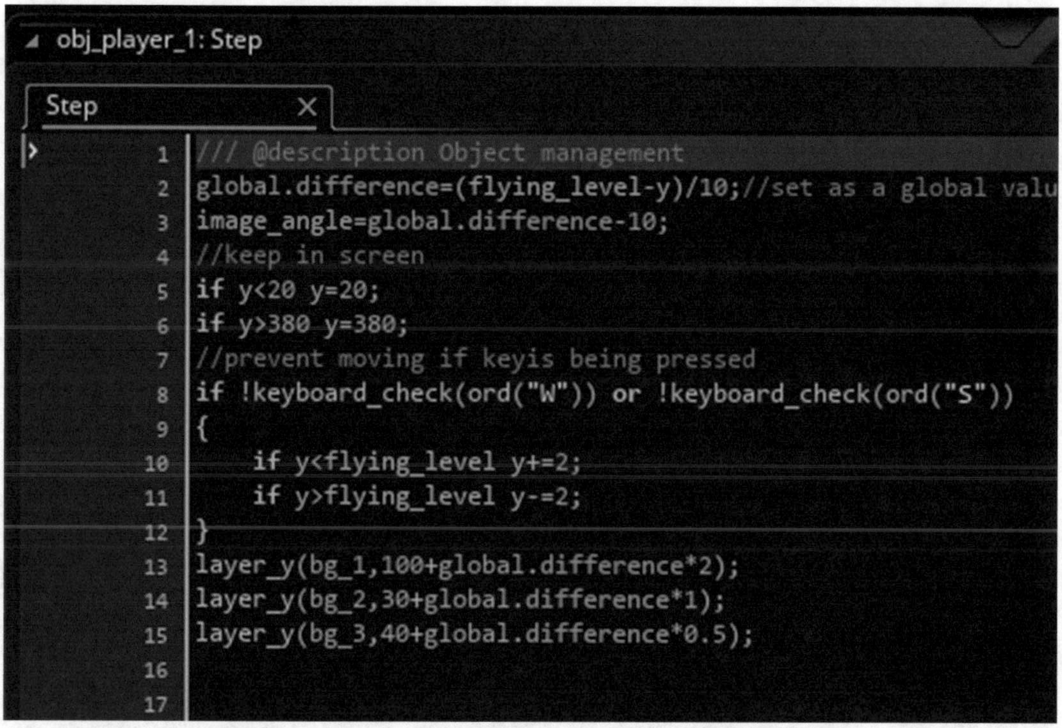
obj_player_1: Step
Step
/// @description Object management
global.difference=(flying_level-y)/10;//set as a global valu
image_angle=global.difference-10;
//keep in screen
if y<20 y=20;
if y>380 y=380;
//prevent moving if keyis being pressed
if !keyboard_check(ord("W")) or !keyboard_check(ord("S"))
{
if y<flying_level y+=2;
if y>flying_level y-=2;
}
layer_y(bg_1,100+global.difference*2);
layer_y(bg_2,30+global.difference*1);
layer_y(bg_3,40+global.difference*0.5);

Figure 5-7. *obj_player_1 Step Event with new code added*

Now is a good point to save and test the game so far.

When you test, it should look like Figure 5-8.

Figure 5-8. *The game in action so far*

The next thing to do is create a firing system for the player. First, load in the spritesheet for the bullet. Let's use a slightly different method than before; once you know both, you can decide which method you prefer. Create a new sprite named **spr_player_bullet** and click Edit Image. Then click Import Strip Image, as shown in Figure 5-9.

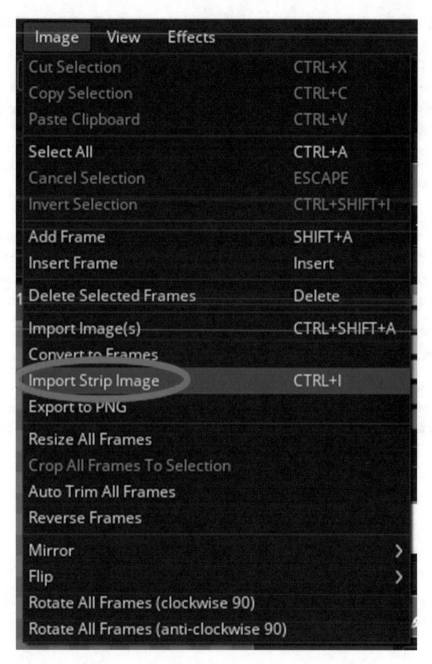

Figure 5-9. *Import the strip image*

Next, select **spr_player_bullet** from the Resources folder. The origin of this sprite is middle center. There are 3 images, each 64x64.

Click Convert to apply these settings.

Create an object called **obj_player_bullet** and set the sprite you just created.

Make a **Create Event** and add the following code to make it move to the mouse's current location at a speed of 6:

```
/// @description Start moving
direction=point_direction(x,y,mouse_x,mouse_y);
speed=6;
```

Next, make an **Outside Room Event** and place the following GML, which destroys itself when outside the room. It's always a good idea to do this with an instance when it's no longer needed because this helps prevent memory leaks, which can slow down and crash your game.

```
/// @description Destroy
instance_destroy();
```

Next, open **obj_player_1** and add a **Mouse Global Left Pressed Event** by clicking Mouse ➤ Global ➤ Global Left Pressed, as shown in Figure 5-10. A **Global Mouse Event** detects a mouse click anywhere in the game window, not just over the object's sprite.

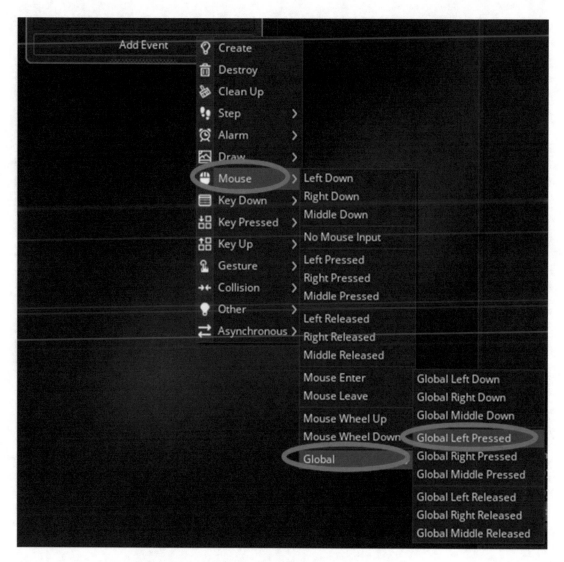

Figure 5-10. *Setting a Global Mouse Left Pressed Event*

The code for this event, which creates a bullet, is

```
/// @description Create a Bullet
instance_create_layer(x,y,"Instances",obj_player_bullet);
```

This is a good point to save and test the game.

If you test the game, you can create bullets by pressing the left mouse button, as shown in Figure 5-11.

Figure 5-11. *Showing progress of the game so far*

One issue you will notice is that you can click really fast and make a barrage of bullets, so let's limit how quickly you can shoot. There are many methods that can be used. Let's use a flag and an alarm. Open up **obj_player_1** and add the following to the current code in the **Create Event**, which allows the player to shoot again:

can_shoot=true;

The **Create Event** code now looks like Figure 5-12.

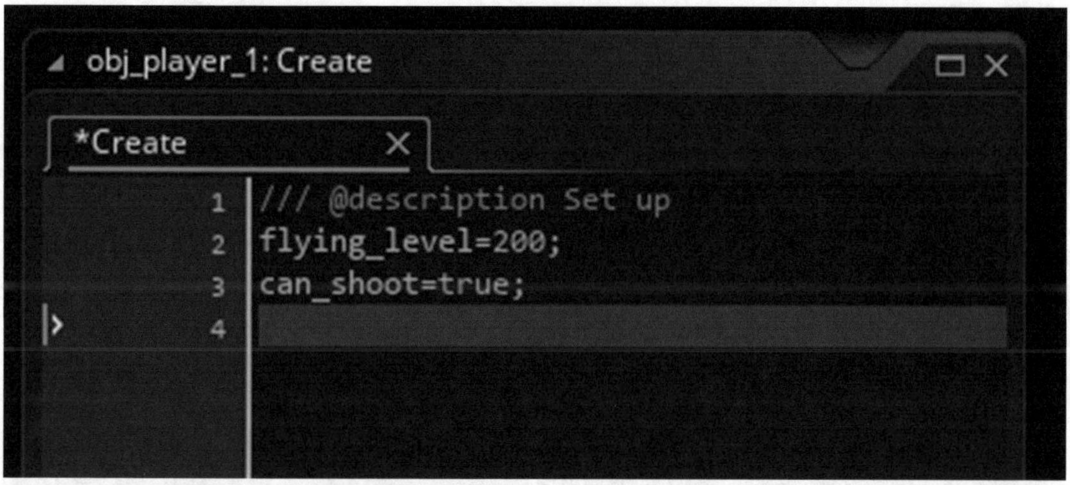

Figure 5-12. *The updated Create Event*

Open the **Global Left Pressed Event** and change the code to the following, which shoots a bullet if **can_shoot** is true, then sets it back to false, and sets an alarm:

```
/// @description Create a Bullet
if can_shoot
{
    can_shoot=false;
    alarm[0]=room_speed;
    instance_create_layer(x,y,"Instances",obj_player_bullet);
}
```

This code allows the player to shoot if the flag is true. It also sets the flag to false to prevent shooting again.

Next, set an **Alarm 0 Event** to set the flag of **can_shoot** back to true via the following code:

```
/// @description Set flag back to true
can_shoot=true;
```

115

Test the game. The shooting speed is limited to once per second!

The next stage is to create an enemy for the player to shoot. Create a sprite named **spr_bat** and load it in from the resources. There are 8 frames, each 64 x 62. Go ahead and load in this sprite sheet.

Since the game will have more than one enemy, create a parent object for all enemies. This allows you to use the code once in the parent, rather than having code in every enemy object.

Create an object named **obj_enemy_parent**. There is no sprite for this object. That is all for this object.

Create an object named **obj_bat** and assign it the sprite **spr_bat** and set the parent object as **obj_enemy_parent**, as shown in Figure 5-13.

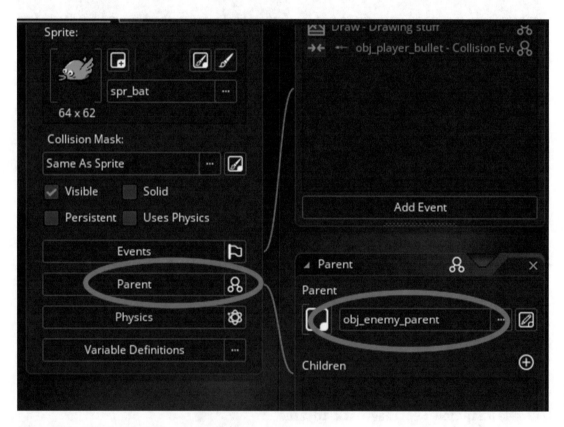

Figure 5-13. *Setting a parent object*

Next, give the bat object some health. You won't use the variable **health** since it is a global variable; instead use an instance variable named **hp**. You also want to set the bat object to move when it's created, so to do both of these actions, put the following code in the **Create Event** of **obj_bat**, which sets its **hp** (health) and its speed to a negative value of **hspeed** to make it move left:

```
/// @description Set HP and move
hp=4;
hspeed=-3;
```

That is all for this object for now.

Next, open the parent object, **obj_enemy_parent**, and enter the following code in the **Step Event**. It destroys the instance if it goes off of the left of the screen. It also destroys the instance if the **hp** is less or equal to 0. The code for doing both actions is the following:

```
/// @description check position and hp
if x<-100
{
    health-=5;
    instance_destroy();
}

if hp<=0
{
    instance_create_layer(x,y,"Effects",obj_enemy_explosion);
    score+=start_hp*10;
    instance_destroy();
}
```

Next, you want a **Collision Event** with **obj_player_bullet**, so add the following code, which reduces **hp** by 1 and destroys the bullet:

```
/// @description Collision Event code
hp-=1;
with (other) instance_destroy();
```

See Figure 5-14.

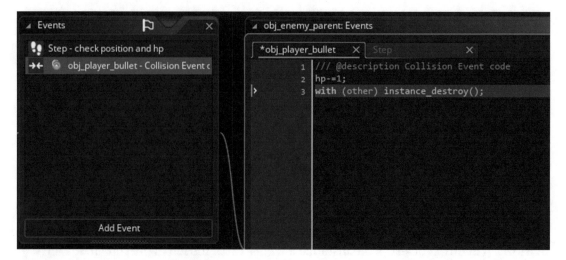

Figure 5-14. *The Collision Event code*

Next up you need a control object to spawn instances of the bat. Create an object named **obj_spawner**. There is no sprite for this object. The **Create Event** code for this object, which sets the alarm to 5 seconds, is as follows:

```
/// @description Start Alarm
alarm[0]=room_speed*5;
```

The **Alarm 0 Event** code, which creates a bat at a y position between 100 and 500 and offscreen at x position 1100, is as follows:

```
/// @description Create instance and restart alarm
var position=irandom_range(100,500);
instance_create_layer(1100,position,"Player",obj_bat);
alarm[0]=room_speed*5;
```

That is all for this object. Place one instance of **obj_spawner** in **room_game**.

Now is great point to save and test the game so far.

If you shoot a bat four times, it will be destroyed.

Next, let's add some graphical effects.

Create a layer for the effects so that they are drawn above other instances. Create a new layer named Effects, as shown in Figure 5-15.

Figure 5-15. *Creating a new layer for effects*

Create a new sprite named **spr_enemy_explosion**, and edit the image. In the Image options, select Import Sprite Sheet. There are 12 frames, each 96 x 96 in size. When done, it will look like Figure 5-16.

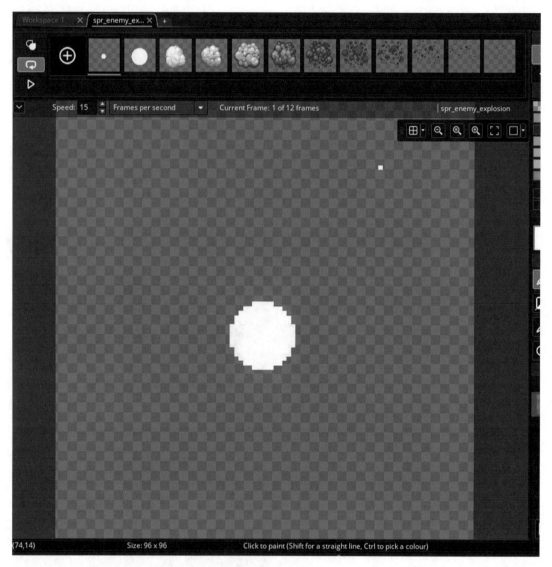

Figure 5-16. *The sprite strip loaded in*

Create an object named **obj_enemy_explosion** and assign it the sprite you just created.

In the **Create Event**, enter the following GML. It sets **image_speed** to 0, preventing animation, and chooses a random sub-image.

```
/// @description Play Sound
audio_play_sound(snd_explosion_1,1,false);
```

In an **Animation End Event,** place the following code, which destroys the instance:

```
/// @description Destroy
instance_destroy();
```

That is all for this object.

If you save and test, you will see the explosion when the bat is destroyed. Note that the player's bullet gets destroyed before it collides with the bat, so let's change the collision mask that detects a **Collision Event**. This mask will be used to check collisions.

Open up **spr_player_bullet**. Open the Collision Mask tab and set it as automatic and rectangle, as shown in Figure 5-17.

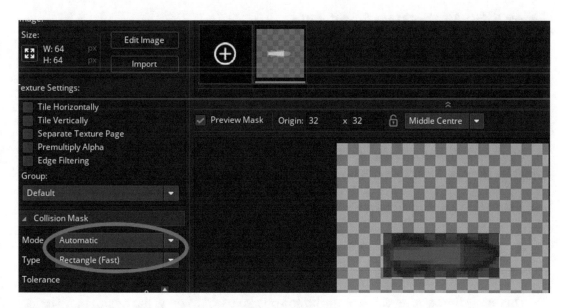

Figure 5-17. *Manually setting a collision mask*

That is all for this sprite. Now open up **spr_bat** and set it as manual and rectangle, as shown in Figure 5-18.

Figure 5-18. *Mask settings for spr_bat*

That is all for this sprite.

You can now save and test. You should notice better collision detection.

The next thing to do is draw a small health bar above the enemy so there is a visual indication of how much **hp** it currently has.

Open up **obj_bat** and change the **Create Event** to the following code, which sets an initial **hp**, the starting **hp** (which is used to draw a healthbar), and the horizontal speed:

```
/// @description Set HP and move
hp=4;
start_hp=hp;
hspeed=-4;
```

This saves the starting value of the **hp** so you can use it to draw the health bar. That is all for this object.

There are several ways to draw a health bar; this is just one method.

Open up **obj_enemy_parent** and change the **Draw Event** code to the following, which draws the sprite and a mini healthbar:

```
/// @description Drawing stuff
draw_self(); //draw current subimage
draw_healthbar(x-40,y-80,x+40,y-60,(100/start_hp)*hp,c_red,c_green,
c_green,0,true,true);
```

That is all for this object.

Next, do something similar for the player object. Open up **obj_player_1** and change the **Create Event** code to the following. At game start, health automatically has a value of 100, but I find it a good practice to define it anyway.

```
/// @description Set up
flying_level=200;
can_shoot=true;
health=100;
```

Make a **Collision Event** with **obj_enemy_parent** and put in the following code, which reduces the player's health if it collides with an enemy:

```
/// @description Reduce health
health--;
```

Finally, set the parent of **obj_bat** to **obj_enemy_parent**, as shown in Figure 5-19. That is all for this object.

Figure 5-19. Showing steps to assign a parent

Create a new object named **obj_hud** and place the following code in a **Draw GUI Event**. It draws the player's healthbar. You could use **draw_healthbar**, but this is an alternative method using rectangles.

```
/// @description Draw HUD

draw_set_colour(c_red);
draw_rectangle(50,500,950,550,false);
draw_set_colour(c_green);
var size=(900/100)*health;
draw_rectangle(50,500,50+size,550,false);
draw_set_colour(c_black);
draw_rectangle(50,500,950,550,true);
```

That is all for this object. Place one instance of it in room_game.

Now is a good time to save and test.

You will see the health bars for the enemy and the player. The enemy will lose **hp** when hit by a bullet, and the player will lose **health** if hits an enemy or an enemy gets past the player. A preview is shown in Figure 5-20.

Figure 5-20. *Showing game in progress so far*

Next, add a new enemy that moves on a path and can shoot at the player.

First, create a sprite for the bullet. For this you will use yet another method.

In the Resource tree, right-click **spr_player_bullet** and select Duplicate, as shown in Figure 5-21.

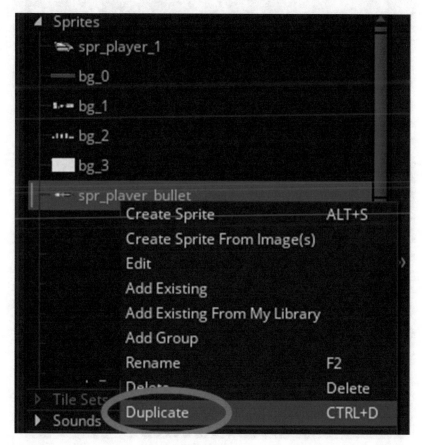

Figure 5-21. *Duplicating an asset in the resource tree*

Name this sprite **spr_enemy_bullet** and set the origin to middle center.

Then click Edit Image. Then click Image ➤ Mirror ➤ All Frames, as shown in Figure 5-22.

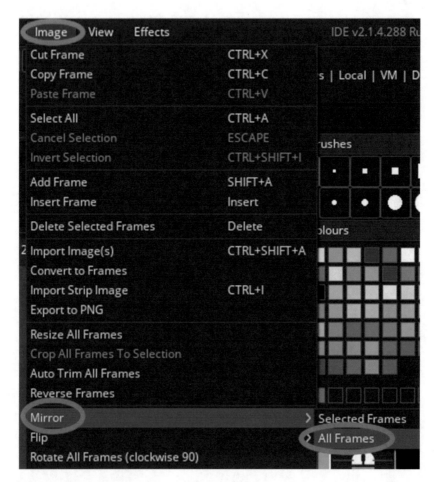

Figure 5-22. *Mirroring a sprite*

Open up **room_game** and create a new path layer, as shown in Figure 5-23. Name it Path_Layer.

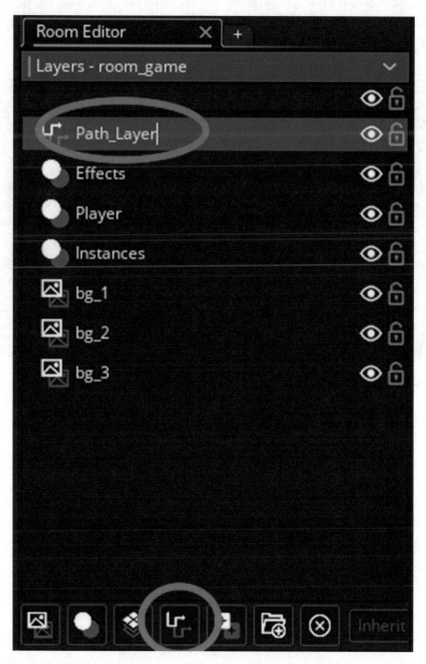

Figure 5-23. *A method to create a new path*

The screen is a little busy right now. Move the Resources tree to one side by clicking the left edge and moving it. Use the Ctrl key and the middle mouse button on the preview window to make it large and show the whole room. Next, hide any layers that you don't need to see right now. Layers can be shown/hidden by clicking the eye icon. Hide all layers except Path_Layer, as shown in Figure 5-24.

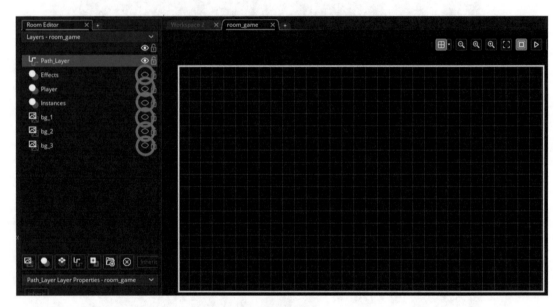

Figure 5-24. *Hiding all layers except Path_Layer*

Now click Select Path ➤ Create New, as shown in Figure 5-25.

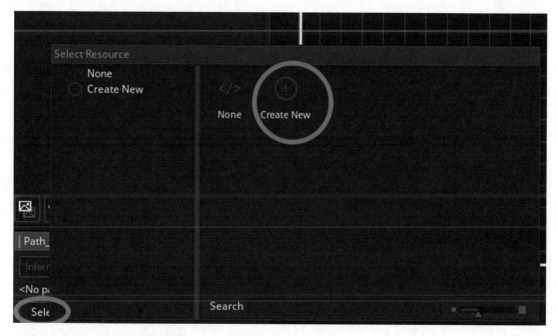

Figure 5-25. *Creating a new path*

Name this path **path_enemy_1**.

Start the path just outside to the right of the room and create a spiral shape, as shown in Figure 5-26. Also check the Smooth Curve option. In this case, it doesn't need to be 100% the same as the example.

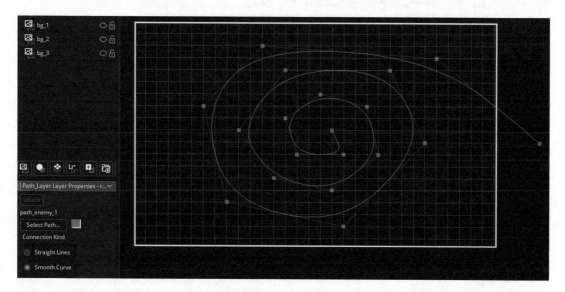

Figure 5-26. *Showing the path and path points, with the smooth curve selected*

That is all for this path.

Next, create a new object named **obj_enemy_bullet** and assign it **spr_enemy_bullet**. In the **Create Event**, enter the following code, which fires a bullet towards the player's current location:

```
/// @description Start moving
direction=point_direction(x,y,obj_player_1.x,obj_player_1.y);
speed=6;
```

In an **Outside Room Event**, enter the following code:

```
/// @description Destroy
instance_destroy();
```

This code has two consequences. First, it destroys itself if it goes past the player to the left and exits the room. It also destroys if it is created when it is outside the room by an enemy object, which prevents the enemy from shooting at the player until it is visible.

Next, create an object that is appears when an enemy bullet hits the player. Create an object named **obj_player_explosion** and assign it a sprite. Duplicate **spr_enemy_explosion** and rename it as **spr_player_explosion**. In the **Create Event**, place the following code, which plays an explosion sound:

```
/// @description Play Sound
audio_play_sound(snd_explosion_2,1,false);
```

In an **Animation End Event**, enter the following code:

```
/// @description Destroy
instance_destroy();
```

You can find the **Animation End Event** at Other ➤ Animation End, as shown in Figure 5-27.

Figure 5-27. *The location of an Animation End Event*

That is for this object.

Now load in the sprite **spr_ufo** and resize it to 128 x 128. Set the origin as middle center.

Create an object named **obj_ufo** and assign it the sprite **spr_ufo**.

In the **Create Event**, enter the following GML to start the instance moving on the path you created and set an alarm, initial **hp** values, and **hspeed**:

```
/// @description Start moving & set alarm - set hp
path_start(path_enemy_1,4,path_action_stop,true);
alarm[0]=room_speed*10;
/// @description Set HP and move
hp=20;
start_hp=hp;
hspeed=-4;
```

In an **Alarm 0 Event**, add code to create a bullet and reset the alarm:

```
/// @description Create bullet and set alarm again
instance_create_layer(x,y,"Effects",obj_enemy_bullet);
alarm[0]=room_speed*10;
```

Set the parent object as **obj_enemy_parent**.

That is all for this object.

Open up object **obj_player_1** and make a **Collision Event** with **obj_enemy_bullet**, and add code to reduce the player's health, create an explosion, and destroy the bullet:

```
/// @description Upon collision
health-=10;
instance_create_layer(x,y,"Effects",obj_player_explosion);
with (other) instance_destroy();
```

Next, open object **obj_spawner** and change the **Create Event** code to the following code, which starts the initial alarms:

```
/// @description Start Alarm
alarm[0]=room_speed*5;
alarm[1]=room_speed*30;
```

Add an **Alarm 1 Event** with code that creates an instance of the UFO enemy at a random position between 100 and 500 and restarts the alarm:

```
/// @description Create instance and restart alarm
position=irandom_range(100,500);
instance_create_layer(1100,position,"Player",obj_ufo);
alarm[0]=room_speed*5;
```

That is all. Now open **room_game**. You need turn the layers back on so they show when the game is played. If you can't see this option, you can always click Room ➤ Reset Windows. When set back on, it should look like Figure 5-28.

Figure 5-28. *Making the layers visible again*

Now is a great point to save and test the game.

Next, you'll create a menu screen, player health and scores, and saving and loading.

First, load in a sprite to be used as a background for the title and Game Over screen. This is **spr_title**.

Create two new rooms, each 1000 x 600 and with **spr_title** set as a background, named **room_title** and **room_game_over**. Change the room order in the Resources tree to that shown in Figure 5-29.

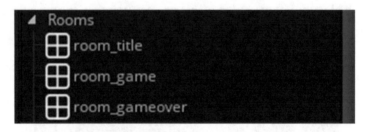

Figure 5-29. *The new order of the rooms*

That is all for the rooms right now.

Next, you need a font to draw info. Create a new font named **font_info** and set it as Arial size 20.

You will be drawing the text a little differently this time. You will create a script that will take in the text to draw and the position and will draw it in red with a black shadow.

Create a new script and name it **draw_text_shadow**.

There is a cool coding trick you can use so the script shows the arguments to use at the bottom of the code window as you type. This can be done with the following code:

```
/// @function draw_text_shadow(xpos, ypos, text)
/// @param {real} xpos
/// @param {real} ypos
/// @param {integer} text
/// @description Draw Text As Shadow
```

The full code script to draw the text with a shadow is

```
/// @function draw_text_shadow(xpos, ypos, text)
/// @param {real} xpos
/// @param {real} ypos
```

```
/// @param {integer} text
/// @description Draw Text As Shadow

draw_set_font(font_info);
draw_set_halign(fa_center);
draw_set_valign(fa_middle);
draw_set_colour(c_black);
draw_text(argument0,argument1,argument2);
draw_set_colour(c_red);
draw_text(argument0+2,argument1+2,argument2);
```

That is all for this script.

Create a new object named **obj_startgame**. No sprite is needed. Add the following code in the **Create Event**:

```
/// @description Load Highscore
ini_open("highscore.ini");
global.highscore=ini_read_real("save","highscore",0);
ini_close();
```

Next, make a **Draw Event** and put the following code in it:

```
/// @description Draw Info
draw_text_shadow(room_width/2,200,"Jet Pack");
draw_text_shadow(room_width/2,240,"Previous Highscore:");
draw_text_shadow(room_width/2,280,global.highscore);
draw_text_shadow(room_width/2,340,"Press To S Start");
```

That is all for this object. Place one instance of it in room **room_title**.

The next object is **obj_gameover**. There is no sprite. It has the following **Create Event** code:

```
/// @description Load Highscore
if score>global.highscore
{
    ini_open("highscore.ini");
    ini_write_real("save","highscore",score);
    ini_close();
}
```

Also, you need a **Draw Event** with the following code:

```
/// @description Show Final Score
draw_text_shadow(room_width/2,220,"Previous Highscore:");
draw_text_shadow(room_width/2,260,global.highscore);
draw_text_shadow(room_width/2,300,"Your Score:");
draw_text_shadow(room_width/2,340,score);
draw_text_shadow(room_width/2,400,"Press To S Restart Game");
```

You also need a **Key Press S Event** with the following code:

```
/// @description Restart Game
game_restart();
```

Place one instance of this object in room **room_gameover**.

The last object to create is a control object for drawing the player's score and monitoring the player's health.

Create an object named **obj_control**. Add a **Step Event** with the following code to check the player's health and take the player to **room_gameover** if 0 or less:

```
/// @description Check Health
if health<=0 room_goto(room_gameover);
```

Add a **Draw GUI Event** with the following code:

```
/// @description Draw Player's score
draw_text_shadow(200,570,"Your Score:");
draw_text_shadow(800,570,score);
```

Place one instance of this object in room **room_game**.

The final step for this game is to add some sound effects.

Load in the sounds now:

- **snd_enemy_shoot**

- **snd_explosion_1**

- **snd_explosion_2**

- **snd_music**

- **snd_no_ammo**

- **snd_player_shoot**

- **snd_you_are_dead**

Add the following code to play **snd_enemy_shoot** in the **Create Event** of object **obj_enemy_bullet**:

```
/// @description Start moving
direction=point_direction(x,y,obj_player_1.x,obj_player_1.y);
speed=6;
audio_play_sound(snd_enemy_shoot,1,false);
```

Add the following code to the **Create Event** of **obj_enemy_explosion**, so it looks like this:

```
/// @description Play Sound
audio_play_sound(snd_explosion_1,1,false);
```

The code for the **Animation End Event** is

```
/// @description Play Sound
audio_play_sound(snd_explosion_1,1,false);
```

This sets the priority to 0 and sets it to play on a loop.

Next, open up **obj_player_1** and change the code in the **Global Left Pressed Event** to

```
/// @description Create a Bullet
if can_shoot
{
    can_shoot=false;
    alarm[0]=room_speed;
    instance_create_layer(x,y,"Instances",obj_player_bullet);
    audio_play_sound(snd_player_shoot,1,false);
}
else
{
    audio_play_sound(snd_no_ammo,1,false);
}
```

This code will play a sound depending on whether the player can currently shoot or not.

Set the final sound named **snd_you_are_dead** to play in the **Create Event** of **obj_gameover** as shown:

```
/// @description Load Highscore & Start Music
if score>global.highscore
{
    ini_open("highscore.ini");
    ini_write_real("save","highscore",score);
    ini_close();
}
audio_play_sound(snd_you_are_dead,1,false);
```

Now you can save and test your game.

Figure 5-30 shows this game in action.

Figure 5-30. *The game in action*

A project file for the completed game is in the Resources folder and it's called **Jet_Pack**.

EXTRA IDEAS FOR YOU TO TRY

1. Keep track of how long the player survives.

2. Make a tank that moves along the bottom and fires at the player.

3. Make a two-player version, with one player on the left and one on the right. The players can shoot at each other.

4. Create an additional weapon that the player can fire with the right mouse button.

5. Make a bonus object that appears after every 10 enemies that the player kills. Award bonus points if the player collects this object.

CHAPTER 6

Darts

In this chapter, you'll create a darts game. This game will continue to build upon what you have learned already. It will also show you more things you can do with paths, ds lists, custom fonts, and by changing the angle of images.

This game is a single-player version of the classic game called 501 Darts. The aim is to score 501 in as few darts as possible, while finishing on a double.

This time, you must perform a task before you start GMS2. Go to the Darts Resources folder and double-click **font_chalk**. Then click Install. This will load the sprite so it can be used by Windows applications.

You can now start GameMaker Studio 2.

This game only has a handful of resources, so let's load them now.

First, add the sprites:

- **spr_dartboard** with the origin set as custom 300 x 346
- **spr_center** with the origin as middle center
- **spr_sight** with the origin as middle center
- **spr_dart** with the origin as custom 2 x 111
- **spr_background** with the origin as default top left

Next are seven sounds:

- **snd_double_points**
- **snd_triple_points**
- **snd_take_cover**
- **snd_perfect**
- **snd_thud_1**
- **snd_thud_2**
- **snd_thud_3**

© Ben Tyers 2018
B. Tyers, *Practical GameMaker Projects*, https://doi.org/10.1007/978-1-4842-3745-8_6

Next, make **font_chalk** and set it as **neatchalk** size 8.

Create a room named **room_game** and add layers named Dart, Path_1, Score, Instances, and Background, as shown in Figure 6-1.

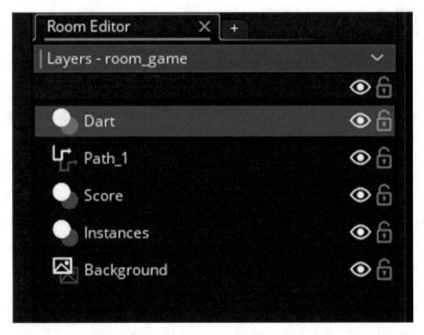

Figure 6-1. *The layers setup*

Go to the Background layer and assign it **spr_bg**.

Next, create the board object, **obj_board**, and assign it the sprite **spr_board**. The origin should be set as center point of the middle of board (center of the red 50 point circle). You do this first so you can see it in the room to enable you to make a path. You won't add any code at this point. Create an object named **obj_board** and place on the Instances layer, as shown in Figure 6-2.

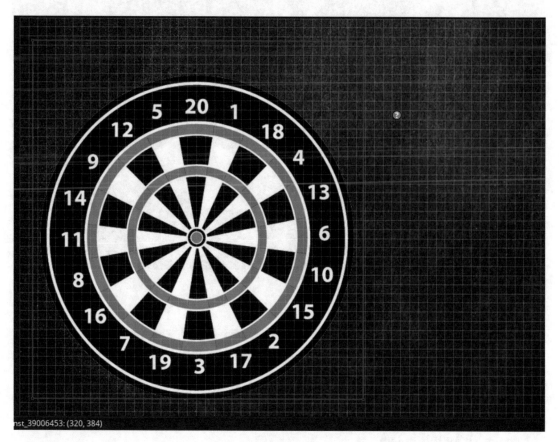

Figure 6-2. *The dartboard placed in the room*

Next, select the Path_1 layer and create a path named **path_circle** that follows the outer edge of the dart board. Set it as a smooth curve and closed, as shown in Figure 6-3.

Figure 6-3. *Showing the path created*

Next, add the following to the **Create Event** of **obj_board**. The item that is created is used as a reference point to determine where on the board the player's dart lands.

```
/// @description Insert Create object at origin
instance_create_layer(x,y,"Instances",obj_center);
```

That is all for this object.

Next, create an object named **obj_control**. There is no sprite for this object. Add a **Create Event** that sets up the initial variables of the game:

```
/// @description Set Up
score=501;
global.go=0;
is_round=true;
is_across=false;
```

```
global.scores=ds_list_create();
ds_list_add(global.scores,501);
global.last=ds_list_create();
text="";

enum state
{
    across,
    circle
}
current=state.circle;
```

Add a **Step Event** that culls a list to keep it at 12 values, gives some info to the player, and checks whether the player has won:

```
/// @description check list size
size=ds_list_size(global.scores);
if size>12
{
    ds_list_delete(global.scores,0);
    ds_list_delete(global.last,0);
}

//set hints text
if (!instance_exists(obj_throw))
{
    text = "Left Click Mouse Button To Start";
}
else
{
    if (current == state.circle)
    {
        text="Click To Stop";
    }
    else if (current == state.across)
    {
```

```
        text="Click To Throw Dart";
    }
}
if score==0
{
    show_message("You Win");
    game_restart();
}
```

Add a **Draw Event** that draws the current throw and previous throws, plus the hint:

```
/// @description Draw Info
draw_set_font(font_chalk);
draw_set_colour(c_white);
draw_set_halign(fa_center);
///draw throw
draw_text(100,20,"Throw = "+string(global.go));
//running total
var size=ds_list_size(global.scores);
for (var i = 0; i < size; i += 1)
{
    draw_text(830,60+(20*i),global.scores[|i]);
}

//previous throws
var size=ds_list_size(global.last);
for (var i = 0; i < size; i += 1)
{
    draw_text(950,60+(20*i),global.last[|i]);
}

draw_text(830,20,"Running Total");
draw_text(950,20,"Throws");

///draw_hints
draw_text(room_width/2,720,text);
```

Add a **Global Left Pressed Mouse Event** that creates an instance of **obj_throw**:

```
/// @description Create a throw
if !instance_exists(obj_throw) && !instance_exists(obj_dart_path);
{
    instance_create_layer(x,y,"Dart",obj_throw);
}
```

That is all for this object. Place one instance of this object on the room's Score layer.

Next is **obj_center**. Assign it **spr_center**. Add a **Create Event** that sets the starting values:

```
/// @description set up
angle=0;
throw=0;
segment=0;
```

Add a **Step Event** that calculates the players depending on where on the board the dart lands:

```
/// @description Calculate throw
if instance_exists(obj_dart)
{
    var type="single";
    angle=(point_direction(x,y,obj_dart.x,obj_dart.y)+8) mod 360;
    var segment=angle div 18;
    var distance=distance_to_point(obj_dart.x,obj_dart.y);
    //get score for segment
    switch (segment)
    {
    case 0:
        pos=6;
        break;
    case 1:
        pos=13;
        break;
    case 2:
        pos=4;
        break;
```

```
case 3:
    pos=18;
    break;
case 4:
    pos=1;
    break;
case 5:
    pos=20;
    break;
case 6:
    pos=5;
    break;
case 7:
    pos=12;
    break;
case 8:
    pos=9;
    break;
case 9:
    pos=14;
    break;
case 10:
    pos=11;
    break;
case 11:
    pos=8;
    break;
case 12:
    pos=16;
    break;
case 13:
    pos=7;
    break;
case 14:
    pos=19;
    break;
```

```
case 15:
    pos=2;
    break;
case 16:
    pos=17;
    break;
case 17:
    pos=2;
    break;
case 18:
    pos=15;
    break;
case 19:
    pos=10;
    break;
}
//get if single, double or  triple
//outside board
if distance>198
{
    throw=0;
    audio_play_sound(snd_take_cover,0,false);
}
else
if distance>=178 && distance<=197
{
    throw=pos*2;
    type="double";
}
else
if distance>=108 && distance<=123
{
    throw=pos*3;
    type="triple";
}
```

```
else
if distance>=9 && distance<=16
{
    throw=25;
}
else
if distance<9
{
    throw=50;
    type="double"; //we use this to check player ends on a double
}else
throw=pos;
//destroy dart
with (obj_dart) instance_destroy();
//calculate new score
if score-throw>=2 // only calculate if 2 or more left on board, so
player must end on a double
{
    score-=throw;
    ds_list_add(global.scores,score);
    ds_list_add(global.last,throw);
    if throw==50 or throw==60
    {
        audio_play_sound(snd_perfect,0,false);

    }
    else if type=="triple"
    {
        audio_play_sound(snd_triple_points,0,false);//play triple if
        not 60
    }
    else if type=="double"
    {
        audio_play_sound(snd_double_points,0,false);
    }
}
```

```
    else if score-throw==0 and type=="double"
    {
            score-=throw;
            ds_list_add(global.scores,score);
            ds_list_add(global.last,throw);
    }
}
else if score==0
{
    show_message("You Win");
    game_restart();
}
```

The next object is **obj_dart_on_board**. Assign it the sprite **spr_dart**. Add a **Create Event** that makes a random angle (+ or –20 degrees) for the dart and sets an alarm:

```
/// @description set up and set alarm
image_angle=image_angle+(irandom_range(-20,20));
alarm[0]=room_speed*4;
```

Add an **Alarm 0 Event** with the following code:

```
/// @description on alarm:
instance_destroy();
```

The next object is **obj_throw**. Assign it **spr_sight**. Add a **Create Event** that starts the object on the circular path you created earlier:

```
/// @description Start in circle
current=state.circle;
path_start(path_circle,12,path_action_continue,true);
```

Add a **Global Left Pressed Event** that creates a path that moves across the board:

```
/// @description upon mouse click:
if current==state.circle
{
    if path_exists(current)
    {
```

```
        path_delete(current);
    }
    path_end();
    current=state.across;
    line=path_add();
    path_add_point(line,x,y,6);
    xx=x-obj_center.x;
    yy=y-obj_center.y;
    path_add_point(line,obj_center.x-xx,obj_center.y-yy,6);
    path_start(line,80,path_action_continue,true);
    exit;
}
if current==state.across
{
    if path_exists(line)
    {
        path_delete(line);
    }
    global.target_x=x;
    global.target_y=y;
    instance_create_layer(x,y,"Dart", obj_dart_path);
    global.go++;
    instance_destroy();
}
```

Finally, add a **Clean Up Event** with the following code:

```
/// @description Remove Paths
if path_exists(current) path_delete(current);
if path_exists(line) path_delete(line);
```

That is all for this object.

Next is **obj_dart**. Assign it **spr_dart**. There is no code for this object.

The final object is **obj_dart_path**. Assign it **spr_dart**. Add a **Create Event** that creates a path that makes it look like the dart is being thrown:

```
/// @description make a path
throw_path=path_add();
path_set_kind(throw_path, 1);
path_set_closed(throw_path, false);
path_add_point(throw_path, room_width, room_height, 50);
path_add_point(throw_path, 600, 60, 50);
path_add_point(throw_path, global.target_x, global.target_y, 50);
path_start(throw_path, 50, path_action_stop, true);
```

Add a **Path Ended Event**, which can be found at Add Event ➤ Other ➤ Path Ended. It places two instances where the dart lands, plays a dart noise, and then destroys itself:

```
/// @description add dart to board
instance_create_layer(global.target_x,global.target_y,"Dart",obj_dart);
instance_create_layer(global.target_x,global.target_y,"Dart",obj_dart_on_
board);
audio_play_sound(choose(snd_thud_1,snd_thud_2,snd_thud_3),0,false);
path_delete(throw_path);
instance_destroy();
```

Add a **Clean Up Event** with the following code:

```
/// @description Clear Memory
if path_exists(throw) path_delete(throw_path);
```

That is all for this game.

Now save and test the game. Figure 6-4 shows this game in action.

Figure 6-4. *The game in action*

A project file for the completed game is in the Resources folder.

EXTRA IDEAS FOR YOU TO TRY

1. Make a two-player version.

2. Currently the game is very accurate. Make it so the dart ends up randomly within 50 pixels of the target area.

3. Make a computer player that can select one of five skill levels.

4. Make a variation of Clock, where the player(s) have to hit numbers 1 to 20 in order.

5. If the player hits treble 20, play some audio and create a graphical effect.

CHAPTER 7

Platform Game

This chapter will introduce some new concepts, the most important of which is using code in a **Step Event** instead of separate events for things like collisions or key presses. It will also show more things you can do with parent objects, and by using sprite control. As per the previous chapter, this game will be made in stages, with save points where you can check the game. To save you time, the sprites have been optimized and are ready to import without changes, other than setting the sprite origins.

The aim of this game is to collect the eggs while losing as few lives as possible.

There are only a few resources for this game, so go ahead and load them in now.

There are three sounds:

- **snd_die**
- **snd_egg**
- **snd_jump**

There is one background: **bg_1**.

The way you will load sprites this time is a little different. If you look at the sprite named **spr_idle_strip4**, you can see that it ends in _strip4. This tells GameMaker how many frames the strip has, and most of the time it gets it right and creates the frames as needed. However, sometimes you may need to manually set the frames.

Go ahead and load the sprites in. The origin of each is middle center, except where noted.

- **spr_player_idle**
- **spr_player_right**
- **spr_player_up**
- **spr_dragonfly**

© Ben Tyers 2018
B. Tyers, *Practical GameMaker Projects*, https://doi.org/10.1007/978-1-4842-3745-8_7

- **spr_snake**

- **spr_ladder**

- **spr_ladder_top**

- **spr_spikes**

- **spr_eggs** with the origin at the bottom of the egg

- **spr_flag**

- **spr_platform**

- **spr_platform_left**

- **spr_platform_right**

- **spr_platform_border**

- **spr_full_mask**

- **spr_change_direction**

Now is a good point to save the game.

Next, create some objects.

Create an object named **obj_platform_parent**; no sprite is needed.

Create another object named **obj_platform_left**, assign it sprite **spr_platform_left**, and set the parent as **obj_platform_parent**, as shown in Figure 7-1.

Figure 7-1. *Assigning the sprite and parent*

Repeat the process for **obj_platform_middle**, **obj_platform_right**, and **obj_platform_border**, remembering to assign the parent object **obj_platform_parent** to them.

Now create a new object named **obj_ladder_parent**; no sprite is needed.

Next, create an object named **obj_ladder_top** and assign it sprite **spr_ladder_top** and parent **obj_ladder_parent**, as shown in Figure 7-2.

Figure 7-2. *obj_ladder_top with its parent set*

Repeat the process for **obj_ladder**, assigning it sprite **spr_ladder** and parent **obj_ladder_parent**.

Next, set up the basics for the player object. Create a new object named **obj_player** and assign it sprite **spr_player_idle**. You will be using three different sprites, which would create different collision masks if you used the default settings. This may cause the player to become stuck and unable to move. To prevent this, you set the sprite named **spr_full_mask** as the collison mask. This step is shown in Figure 7-3.

Figure 7-3. *Setting spr_full_mask as the collision mask*

In a **Create Event**, add code to set some initial variables for the player:

```
/// @description Set Up Player

vsp = 0;
hsp = 0;
grav = 0.3;
grounded = 0;
flip = 1;
djump = 0;
ladder = false;
image_speed=0.5;
x_respawn=x;
y_respawn=y;
```

Then make a **Step Event**. This time around, use GML code to detect keypresses within the **Step Event**, rather than using separate events for each key. Place the following in a **Step Event** to do the movement and sprite control for the player:

159

```
/// @description Movement Code
//Get our inputs
var Key_Left=keyboard_check_direct(vk_left);
var Key_Right=keyboard_check_direct(vk_right);
var Key_Jump=keyboard_check_pressed(vk_space);
var Key_Up=keyboard_check_direct(vk_up);
var Key_Down=keyboard_check_direct(vk_down);
if Key_Left or Key_Right
{
    sprite_index=spr_player_right;
}
else
{
    sprite_index=spr_player_idle
}
//Move left and right
if Key_Left
{
    hsp=-2;
    flip=-1;
}

if Key_Right
{
    hsp=2;
    flip=1;
}

//Neutral input = 0 movement
if (Key_Right && Key_Left) or (!Key_Right && !Key_Left)
{
    hsp=0;
}

//Jumping
if (Key_Jump)
{
```

```
    audio_play_sound(snd_jump,0,false);
    if (grounded)
    {
        vsp=-6;
    }
    else
    {
        if(djump)
        {
            vsp=-6;
            djump=0;
        }
    }
}

vsp +=grav;

//Ladder
if Key_Up || Key_Down
{
    if place_meeting(x,y,obj_ladder_parent)
    {
        ladder = true;
    }
}

if ladder
{
    vsp=0;
    if Key_Up
    {
        vsp=-2;
    }
    if Key_Down
    {
        vsp=2;
    }
```

```
    if !place_meeting(x,y,obj_ladder_parent)
    {
        ladder=false;
    }
    if (Key_Jump)
    {
        ladder=false;
    }
    sprite_index=spr_player_up;
    if Key_Up or Key_Down
    {
        image_speed=0.5;
    }
    else
    {
        image_speed=0; //if on ladder and moving animate sprite else set to 0
    }
}
else //allow regular animation when off ladder
{
    image_speed=0.5;
}

//Horizontal Collision
if place_meeting(x+hsp,y,obj_platform_parent)
{
    while (!place_meeting(x+sign(hsp),y,obj_platform_parent))
    {
        x+=sign(hsp);
    }
    hsp=0;
}
x+=hsp;
```

```
//Vertical Collision
if place_meeting(x,y+vsp,obj_platform_parent)
{
    while (!place_meeting(x,y+sign(vsp),obj_platform_parent))
    {
        y+=sign(vsp);
    }
    if (sign(vsp)==1)
    {
        grounded=1;
        djump=1;
    }
    vsp=0;
}
else
{
    grounded=0;
}
y+=vsp;
```

That is all for now for this object. You will come back to it again later.

Create a room named **room_game** and set background **bg_1** to the Background layer and set it to stretch.

Place some instances on the Instances layer, as shown in Figure 7-4.

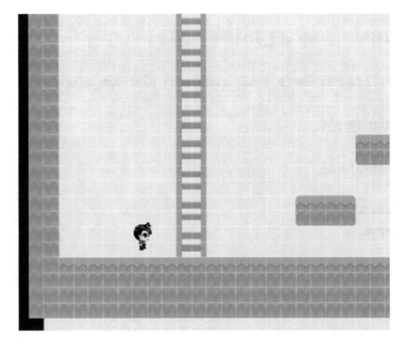

Figure 7-4. *A testing level*

Now is a good time to save and test the game.

Next, create the main aim of the game, which is to collect eggs. Create an object named **obj_egg** and assign the sprite **spr_egg**. In the **Create Event**, add the following code to set a random subimage:

```
/// @description set random starting sub image and prevent animation
image_index=irandom(1);
image_speed=0;
```

That is all for this object.

Next, detect a collision with **obj_egg**. You won't use a **Collision Event** for this; instead you will use code with the player object's **Step Event**. Open up **obj_player** and add the following below the current code in the **Step Event**. This code destroys the egg and plays a sound effect:

```
//egg collision
var egg;
egg=instance_place(x,y,obj_egg);
if egg!= noone
```

```
{
    with (egg) instance_destroy(egg);
    audio_play_sound(snd_egg,0,false);
}
```

That is all for now.

Open up **room_game** and make a new Instances layer named Items. Place it under the current Instances layer. Add some eggs to the level for the player to collect.

Next, create an object that will be used as a respawn point. Create an object named **obj_flag** and assign it the **spr_flag**. That is all for this object.

Open up object **obj_player** and add the following code under the current code in the **Step Event**. This code remembers the last location where the player collided with **obj_flag** and respawns the player after death:

```
//flag respawn point collision
if place_meeting(x,y,obj_flag)
{
    x_respawn=x;
    y_respawn=y;
    show_debug_message("Met Flag");
}
```

This code indicates that it is working by displaying a message in the output box.

You don't yet have any enemies to make the respawn happen, so create a **Key Pressed R Event** in **obj_player**, with the following code, so you can tell that it all works as intended:

```
/// @description for testing
x=x_respawn;
y=y_respawn;
```

Place a few instances of **obj_egg** and **obj_flag** on the Items layer in **room_game**, as shown in Figure 7-5.

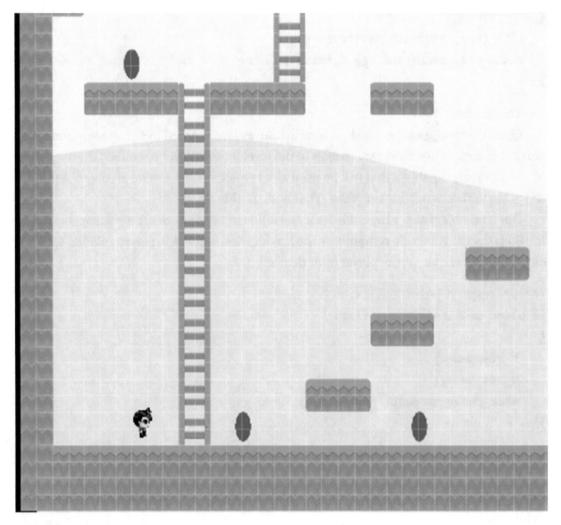

Figure 7-5. *A test layout*

Now save and test the game so far.

Check that you can collect the eggs. Also test that, upon pressing Enter, you return to the last flag point.

Next, you will create some enemy objects.

First, however, you must create an object that makes the enemies change direction. Create an object named **obj_change_direction**; assign it sprite **spr_change_direction** and uncheck the Visible option so that it won't be seen when the game is played, as shown in Figure 7-6.

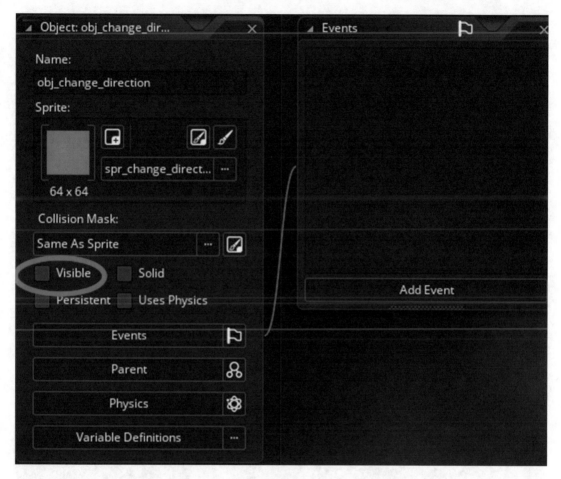

Figure 7-6. *Setting the object sprite and unchecking the Visible option*

That is all for this object.

Next, create an object named **obj_enemy_parent**. Set the mask to **spr_full_mask**. In a **Create Event**, add the following code to start the enemy moving:

```
/// @description Start Moving
motion_set(0,3);
```

In a **Step Event**, enter the following GML. It makes the instance change direction and flips the sprite so it faces in the direction:

```
/// @description Detect Collision
if instance_place(x,y,obj_change_direction)
```

CHAPTER 7   PLATFORM GAME

```
{
    hspeed*=-1;
    image_xscale*=-1;
}
```

That is all for this object.

Now create an object named **obj_enemy_snake** and assign its parent as **obj_enemy_parent** and sprite as **spr_snake**.

Create an object named **obj_enemy_dragonfly** and assign its parent as **obj_enemy_parent** and sprite as **spr_dragonfly**.

Create an object named **obj_spike;** it does not have a parent but it does have a sprite: **spr_spike**.

Open the room and place some instances of **obj_change_direction** and a few of **obj_dragon_fly**.

Because the sprite for **obj_enemy_snake** is a different size than the other sprites, you must change some room settings in order to place it over the platform objects without a gap. Change the grid snap settings to 32 x 8, as shown in Figure 7-7.

Figure 7-7. *The new grid snap settings*

Place an instance of the snake and **obj_spike** as shown in the test layout in Figure 7-8.

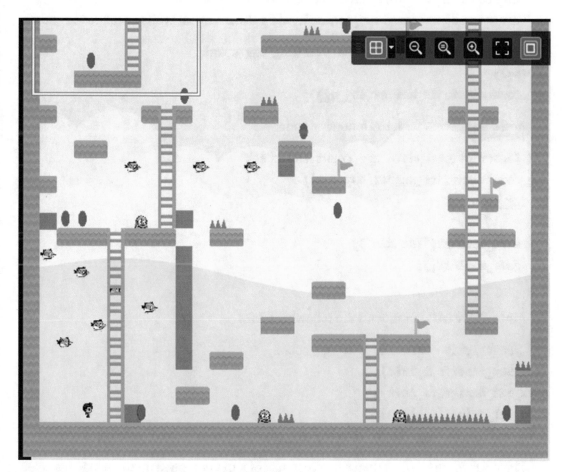

Figure 7-8. *A test layout*

Next, make it so the player dies if it hits an enemy. Add the following code under the current code in the **obj_player's** Step Event:

```
//collision with enemy
if place_meeting(x,y,obj_enemy_parent) or place_meeeting(x,y,obj_spike)
{
    x=x_respawn;
    y=y_respawn;
    lives++;
    audio_play_sound(snd_die,0,false);}
```

Lastly, create an object to show how many lives the player has used and how many eggs are left.

You need a font for this, so create **font_info** in Arial size 22.

Create an object named **obj_control**. Add a **Create Event** with the following code:

```
/// @description set lives and starting egg count
lives=1;
egg_count=instance_number(obj_egg);
```

Add a **Step Event** with the following code:

```
/// @description Update egg count and check
egg_count=instance_number(obj_egg);
if egg_count==0
{
    show_message("You Win");
    game_restart();
}
```

Add a **Draw GUI Event** with the following GML:

```
/// @description Draw lives & egg count
draw_set_font(font_info);
draw_set_halign(fa_left);
draw_set_colour(c_black);
draw_text(50,50,"Eggs Left:"+string(egg_count)+"Lives Taken:"+string(lives));
```

That is all for this object. Place one instance of it in **room_game** on the Instances layer.

Next, create a new Instances layer called Player and put this at the top of the layers. This layer is used just for the player object, ensuring that it is drawn above everything else. Place an instance of **obj_player** on this layer, remembering to remove it from the previous layer.

Now is a great point to save and test the game.

Figure 7-9 shows the game in progress.

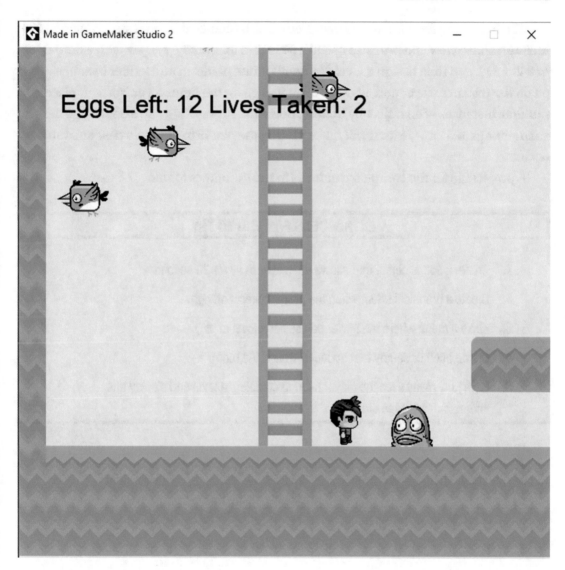

Figure 7-9. *The game in action*

The final thing for this game is to design a level. Change the room size to 2000 x 2000. Make an active view and port size of 640 x 640 set to follow **obj_player** with a border or 240 x 240, and then design a level. Remember that platform and ladder instances go on the Instances layer and all other instances go on the Items layer. You can place multiple instances of an object by holding down the Alt key. You can also change the grid snap settings to 64 x 64, which will make placing the platform objects easier and more accurate.

A project file for the completed game is in the Resources folder.

EXTRA IDEAS FOR YOU TO TRY

1. Create a bonus object that allows the player to fly for 20 seconds.

2. Create a graphical effect when the player collects an egg.

3. Make a menu where the player can select a level to play.

4. Create another enemy that bounces around the room.

5. Save how many lives the player used to complete a level and display this information on game start.

CHAPTER 8

Bomber

This game you will make in this chapter is a remake of the classic bomber game. It will introduce more GML coding, creating paths on the fly, and other cool features.

There are two aims to this game: collect the fruit and destroy the enemy. You can collect ammo, which you can then try to drop on the enemy. However, you can be damaged by your own as well as enemy bombs.

First, load in the assets needed.

Load in the following sprites; the origin of each is middle center unless indicated otherwise. Another way of importing sprites is to right-click Sprites in the Resources tree and select Create Sprite.

- **bg_1**
- **spr_block** with an origin of top left
- **spr_bomb_crate**
- **spr_bomb_ticking**
- **spr_e_move_down**
- **spr_e_move_left**
- **spr_e_move_right**
- **spr_e_move_up**
- **spr_explosion**
- **spr_fruit**
- **spr_p_idle_down**
- **spr_p_idle_left**
- **spr_p_idle_right**

© Ben Tyers 2018
B. Tyers, *Practical GameMaker Projects*, https://doi.org/10.1007/978-1-4842-3745-8_8

- **spr_p_idle_up**

- **spr_p_move_down**

- **spr_p_move_left**

- **spr_p_move_right**

- **spr_p_move_up**

Things are a little busy, so let's tidy up a bit. Right-click Sprites and select Add Group, as shown in Figure 8-1.

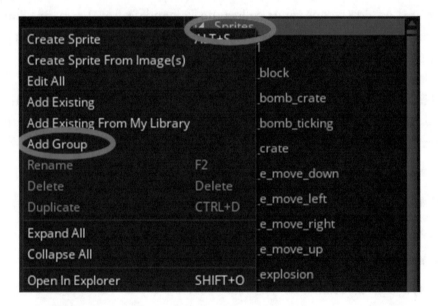

Figure 8-1. *Creating a group*

Create three groups (player, enemy, and other) and then drag the resources into those groups. When done, it will look like Figure 8-2. You can expand/collapse groups by clicking the small triangle.

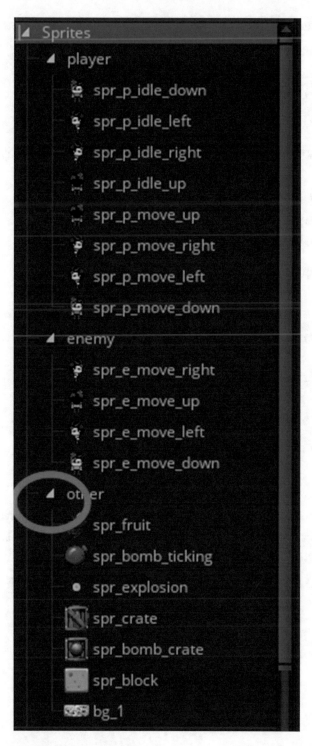

Figure 8-2. *The Resource tree with groups*

Next, set up a script named **scr_move_object**. It is used to process the player's movements. The code is as follows:

```
/// @function scr_move_object(dx,dy)
/// @param {real} xpos
/// @param {real} ypos

// Attempts to move the current instance, pushing things around as needed.

// calculate new coordinates:
var dx=argument0,nx=x+dx;
var dy=argument1,ny=y+dy;

if (place_meeting(nx,ny,obj_block))
{
    // if there's a wall there, definitely can't move there
    return false;
}
else if (place_free(nx,ny))
{
    // if there's nothing there, just move there
    x=nx; y=ny;
    return true;
}
```

Next, set up some basic movements and sprite control for the player.

Create an object named **obj_block** and assign it the sprite **spr_block**. There is no code for this object.

Next, create **obj_player** and assign it **spr_idle_down**. Add a **Create Event** and enter the following code:

```
/// @description Set Up
bombs=5;
move_dx=0;
move_dy=0;
move_amt=0;
image_index=0;
image_speed=0;
```

```
spawnedextra1=false;
spawnedextra2=false;
spawnedextra3=false;
///move control set up
enum player_state
{
    idle,
    up,
    down,
    left,
    right
}

dir=player_state.down;
is_moving=false;
image_speed=0.5;
```

Next, add a **Step Event** that takes care of the player's movement and sets the appropriate sprite based on which key is being pressed:

```
/// @description Player Movement & Sprite Control
//get keypresses
var key_left=keyboard_check(vk_left) ;
var key_right=keyboard_check(vk_right)
var key_up=keyboard_check(vk_up)
var key_down=keyboard_check(vk_down)
var key_shoot=keyboard_check_pressed(ord("Z"))

if (move_amt > 0)
{
    // moving towards destination
    if (scr_move_object(move_dx, move_dy))
    {
        move_amt -= 1;
    }
    else move_amt = 0; // if hit a wall, stop moving
}
```

```
else
{
    var spd = 4; // movement speed (grid size should divide by it w/o remainder)
    move_amt = 64 div spd; // calculate number of steps for movement
    move_dx = 0;
    move_dy = 0;
    if key_left && !position_meeting(x-40,y,obj_block)
    {
        move_dx = -spd;
        dir=player_state.left;
        is_moving=true;
    }
    else if key_right && !position_meeting(x+40,y,obj_block)
    {
        move_dx = spd;
        dir=player_state.right;
        is_moving=true;
    }
    else if key_up && !position_meeting(x,y-40,obj_block)
    {
        move_dy = -spd;
        dir=player_state.up;
        is_moving=true;
    }
    else if key_down && !position_meeting(x,y+40,obj_block)
    {
        move_dy = spd;
        dir=player_state.down;
        is_moving=true;
    }
    else
    {
        move_amt = 0; // don't move if no buttons are pressed
        is_moving=false;
    }
}
```

```
//set is_moving to true if no keypress but still moving to target position
if xprevious!=x or yprevious!=y is_moving=true;
///animation
if is_moving
{
    switch (dir)
    {
        case player_state.up:
        sprite_index=spr_p_move_up;
        break;

        case player_state.down:
        sprite_index=spr_p_move_down;
        break;

        case player_state.left:
        sprite_index=spr_p_move_left;
        break;

        case player_state.right:
        sprite_index=spr_p_move_right;
        break;
    }
}
else
{
    switch (dir)
    {
        case player_state.up:
        sprite_index=spr_p_idle_up;
        break;

        case player_state.down:
        sprite_index=spr_p_idle_down;
        break;

        case player_state.left:
        sprite_index=spr_p_idle_left;
        break;
```

```
    case player_state.right:
    sprite_index=spr_p_idle_right;
    break;
  }
}
```

Make a room named **room_game** and set it up for testing, as shown in Figure 8-3. Now is a good point to save and test your game.

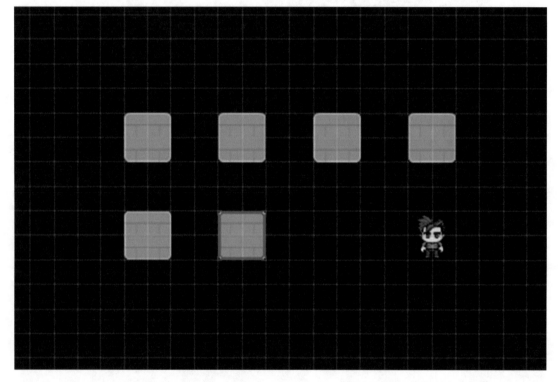

Figure 8-3. *A level set up for testing*

Next, create some bombs and explosions.

Create a new layer in the **room_game** called bomb. Place it above the Instances layer.

Create a font named **font_bomb** using Arial size 8.

First, create a sound named **snd_explosion** from the Resources folder.

Next, create an object named **obj_explosion** and assign it **spr_explosion**.

Create an **Animation End Event** by clicking Add Event ➤ Other ➤ Animation End, as shown in Figure 8-4.

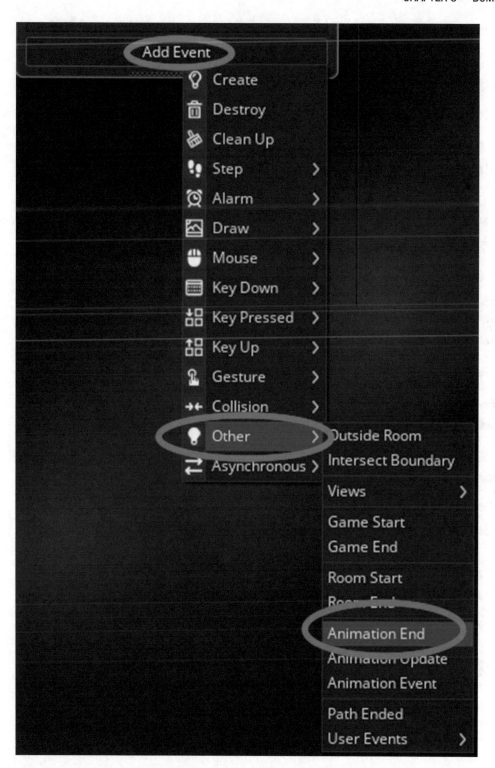

Figure 8-4. *Setting an Animation End Event*

Place the following code in this event:

```
/// @description Destroy
instance_destroy();
```

Next, make a **Create Event** and add this code:

```
/// @description Play Explosion Sound
audio_play_sound(snd_explosion,0,false);
```

That is all for this object.

Next, create an object named **obj_bomb** and assign it the sprite **spr_bomb_ticking**.

Add a **Create Event** with the following code:

```
/// @description snap, set life and alarm
move_snap(32,32);
life=8;
alarm[0]=room_speed/4;
```

Add an **Alarm 0 Event** with the following code:

```
life--;
alarm[0]=room_speed/4;
```

The **Step Event** holds code to create an explosion instance in four directions, if the place doesn't have a block in it, like so:

```
/// @description Create explosion in empty space
if life==0
{
    //create exp at position
    instance_create_layer(x,y,"bomb",obj_explosion);

    //create up
    if !position_meeting(x,y-64,obj_block)
    {
        instance_create_layer(x,y-64,"bomb",obj_explosion);
        if !position_meeting(x,y-128,obj_block)
        {
```

```
        instance_create_layer(x,y-128,"bomb",obj_explosion);
        if !position_meeting(x,y-192,obj_block)
        {
            instance_create_layer(x,y-192,"bomb",obj_explosion);
        }
    }
}
//create down
if !position_meeting(x,y+64,obj_block)
{
    instance_create_layer(x,y+64,"bomb",obj_explosion);
    if !position_meeting(x,y+128,obj_block)
    {
        instance_create_layer(x,y+128,"bomb",obj_explosion);
        if !position_meeting(x,y+192,obj_block)
        {
            instance_create_layer(x,y+192,"bomb",obj_explosion);
        }
    }
}
//create left
if !position_meeting(x-64,y,obj_block)
{
    instance_create_layer(x-64,y,"bomb",obj_explosion);
    if !position_meeting(x-128,y,obj_block)
{
    instance_create_layer(x-128,y,"bomb",obj_explosion);
    if !position_meeting(x-192,y,obj_block)
    {
        instance_create_layer(x-192,y,"bomb",obj_explosion);
    }
}
}
```

```
//create right
if !position_meeting(x+64,y,obj_block)
{
    instance_create_layer(x+64,y,"bomb",obj_explosion);
    if !position_meeting(x+128,y,obj_block)
    {
        instance_create_layer(x+128,y,"bomb",obj_explosion);
        if !position_meeting(x+192,y,obj_block)
        {
            instance_create_layer(x+192,y,"bomb",obj_explosion);
        }
    }
}
instance_destroy();
}
//set off bomb if hit by explosion
if position_meeting(x,y,obj_explosion)
{
    life=0;
}
```

Add a **Draw Event** with the following code:

```
/// @description Draw sprite & countdown
draw_set_halign(fa_center);
draw_set_valign(fa_middle)
draw_set_colour(c_red);
draw_set_font(font_bomb);
draw_self();
draw_text(x,y,life);
```

Finally, add the following code to the bottom of the current code in the player's **Step Event**, creating a bomb at the present location if the player has any bombs:

```
///create a bomb if player has some
if key_shoot && bombs>0
{
```

```
    bombs-=1;
    instance_create_layer(x,y,"bomb",obj_bomb);
}
```

Now is a good point to save and test the game.

Next, we'll create some items for the players to collect.

Create an object named **obj_fruit** and assign it the sprite **spr_fruit**.

Add a **Create Event** with code for choosing a random sub-image and placing it in a free location:

```
/// @description Insert choose random sub-image and jump to free position
image_index=irandom(image_number-1);
image_speed=0;
do
{
    var xx=(random(room_width) div 64) * 64+32;
    var yy =(random(room_height) div 64) * 64+32;
}
until (place_free(xx, yy));
x=xx;
y=yy;
```

That is all for this object.

Next, create an object named **obj_bomb_crate** and assign it the sprite **spr_bomb_crate**.

Add **Create Event** with the following code:

```
/// @description jump to free position
do
{
    var xx=(random(room_width) div 64) * 64+32;
    var yy=(random(room_height) div 64) * 64+32;
}
until (place_empty(xx, yy));
x=xx;
y=yy;
```

That is all for this object.

In order to detect a free position, you need to make **obj_block**, solid, open it, and set it as visible and solid, as shown in Figure 8-5.

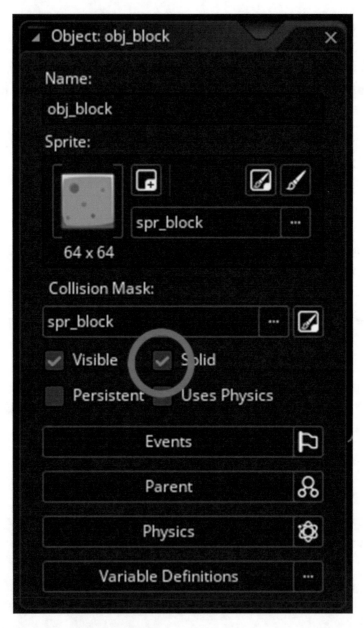

Figure 8-5. *Setting an object to solid*

Next, set up some **Collision Events** for **obj_player**. You could do this in code, but to keep things tidy and easy to understand, you will use **Collision Events**. There is nothing wrong with using **Collision Events** instead of code.

Load in the sounds named **snd_collect_item** and **snd_collect_bomb**.

Open **obj_player** and make a **Collision Event** with **obj_fruit**; it has the following code:

```
/// @description Permorm Collision code
score+=100;
with (other) instance_destroy();
instance_create_layer(5,5,"bomb",obj_fruit);
audio_play_sound(snd_collect_item,0,false);
```

Next, make a **Collision Event** with **obj_bomb_crate** that contains the following code:

```
/// @description Perform Collision code
bombs+=5;
if bombs>10 bombs=10;
with (other) instance_destroy();
instance_create_layer(5,5,"bomb",obj_bomb_crate);
audio_play_sound(snd_collect_bomb,0,false);
```

Next, make a **Collision Event** with **obj_explosion** with code that sets a flag and alarm, and reduces health by 1 for each frame that the player collides with:

```
/// @description Lose Health
health--;
```

That is all for now.

Open room **room_game** and design it as shown in Figure 8-6. Ensure that the blocks are on the Instances level.

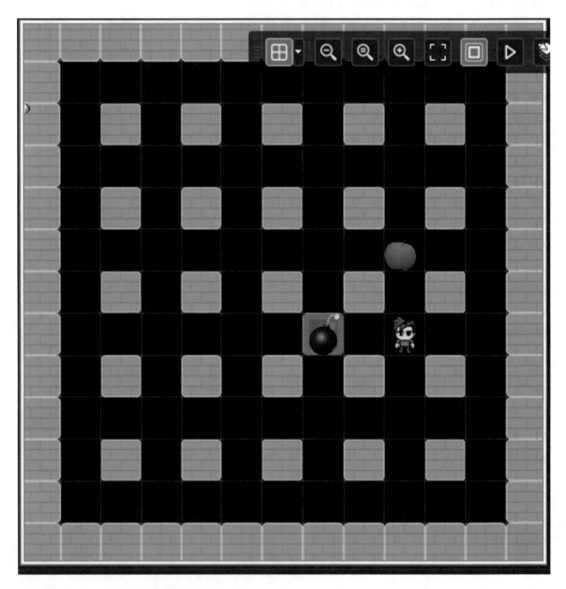

Figure 8-6. *A level for testing*

Note that all of the instances are snapped to a 64 x 64 grid, as shown in Figure 8-7.

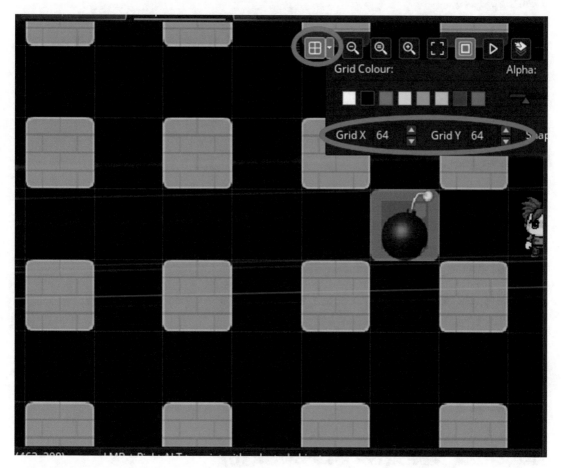

Figure 8-7. *Close-up of placed instances*

Now is a good point to save and test the game so far.

Next, create a computer player for the player to play against.

Create an object named **obj_enemy** and assign it **spr_e_move_down**.

In a **Create Event**, add the following code. The first part sets a grid that marks off instances of **obj_block** so the enemy cannot move there. It then creates a path to the fruit, crate, or player and starts that path. Finally, it sets initial values and starts an alarm (which is used to drop bombs).

```
/// @description Setup
//set up grid
size=64;
grid = mp_grid_create(0,0,ceil(room_width/size),ceil(room_height/size),
size,size);
set_up_grid=true;
mp_grid_add_instances(grid,obj_block,false)
```

```
///create path
path=path_add();
do
{
    choose_target=choose(obj_fruit,obj_bomb_crate,obj_player);
}
until distance_to_object(choose_target)>240
```

```
mp_grid_path(grid,path,x,y,choose_target.x,choose_target.y,false);
path_start(path,4,path_action_stop,true);
//score
enemy_score=0;
enemy_hp=100;
enemy_bombs=5;
```

```
//Start bomb drop alarm
alarm[1]=room_speed*3+(room_speed*irandom(5));
```

In a **Step Event**, enter GML that sets the sprite for the direction it is moving:

```
/// @description Basic control of sprites
ang=round(direction/90)*90;
if ang==0 or ang==360 sprite_index=spr_e_move_right;
if ang==90 sprite_index=spr_e_move_up;
if ang==180 sprite_index=spr_e_move_left;
if ang==270 sprite_index=spr_e_move_down;
```

In an **Alarm 1 Event**, add GML that creates a bomb (if the enemy has any) and resets the alarm:

```
/// @description Create bombs
if enemy_bombs>0
{
    enemy_bombs--;
    instance_create_layer(x,y,"bomb",obj_bomb)
}
alarm[1]=room_speed*3+(room_speed*irandom(5));
```

In a **Collision Event** with **obj_bomb_crate**, add the code that increases the enemy's bomb inventory by 5 (up to a maximum of 5), creates a new bomb crate, and plays a sound:

```
/// @description Perform Collision code
enemy_bombs+=5;
if enemy_bombs>10 enemy_bombs=10;
with (other) instance_destroy();
instance_create_layer(5,5,"bomb",obj_bomb_crate);
audio_play_sound(snd_collect_bomb,0,false);
```

In a **Collision Event** with **obj_explosion**, enter the following code:

```
/// @description reduce health
enemy_hp--;
```

In a **Collision Event** with **obj_fruit**, enter the following code:

```
/// @description Permorm Collision code
enemy_score+=100;
with (other) instance_destroy();
instance_create_layer(5,5,"bomb",obj_fruit);
audio_play_sound(snd_collect_item,0,false);
```

And in a **Path Ended Event**, add the code below that makes a new path and starts the enemy on it:

```
/// @description Choose a new target
path_clear_points(path);
choose_target=choose(obj_fruit,obj_bomb_crate,obj_player);
mp_grid_path(grid,path,x,y,choose_target.x,choose_target.y,false);
path_start(path,5,path_action_stop,true);
```

Finally, add a **Clean Up Event** with the following code to free any memory used by the grid and path:

```
/// @description Clean Up
path_delete(path);
my_grid_destroy(grid);
```

Add an instance of **obj_enemy** into the room in an empty area.

Finally, make a control object to show game details and check for a winner.

Create a font named **font_info** as Arial size 14.

Create an object named **obj_control**. In a **Create Event**, add the following code:

```
/// @description Set up lives
player_lives=10;
enemy_lives=10;
```

In a **Step Event**, add the following code:

```
/// @description Check health and lives
if obj_enemy.enemy_hp<0
{
    enemy_lives--;
    obj_enemy.enemy_hp=100;
}
if health<0
{
    player_lives--;
    health=100;
}
```

```
/// @description Check For Winner
if enemy_lives==0
{
    show_message("Player Wins");
    game_restart();
}
if player_lives==0
{
    show_message("Enemy Wins");
    game_restart();
}
```

In a **Draw GUI Event**, add the following code:

```
/// @description Drawing
draw_set_colour(c_black);
draw_set_font(font_info);
draw_set_halign(fa_center);
draw_set_valign(fa_middle);
//draw player stuff
draw_healthbar(10,10,758,30,health,c_blue,c_red,c_green,0,true,true);
draw_text(200,20,"Player Score:"+string(score));
draw_text(400,20,"Bombs:"+string(obj_player.bombs));
draw_text(600,20,"Lives:"+string(player_lives));
//draw enmey stuff
draw_healthbar(10,718,758,738,obj_enemy.enemy_hp,c_blue,c_red,
c_green,0,true,true);
draw_text(200,728,"Enemy Score:"+string(obj_enemy.enemy_score));
draw_text(400,728,"Bombs:"+string(obj_enemy.enemy_bombs));
draw_text(600,728,"Lives:"+string(enemy_lives));
```

That is all for this object. Place one instance of it in the room.

Figure 8-8 shows this game in action.

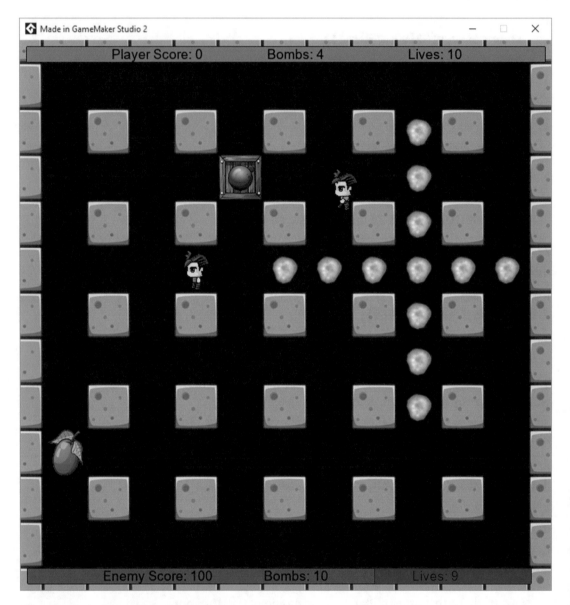

Figure 8-8. *The game in action*

A project file for the completed game is in the Resources folder.

EXTRA IDEAS FOR YOU TO TRY

1. Make a two-player version.

2. Make a larger play area and set it to keep both player and enemy in the current camera view.

3. Make a super bomb that appears very occasionally. Allow player/enemy to drop it. Make the explosion distance twice that of a regular bomb.

4. Create extra blocks that are placed randomly in the areas where the player can move. If these blocks are hit by an explosion three times, destroy them.

5. Set it up so a player can play with a gamepad.

CHAPTER 9

Match 3

The little game you'll make in this chapter is a basic remake of the classic Match 3 game. The aim of the game is to match three or more of the same sweet, which is done by swapping over adjacent sweets.

This game makes use of just six sprites, so go ahead and load them in now:

- **spr_block** (which is a strip of seven images, 32 x 32)
- **spr_border**
- **spr_make_move**
- **spr_please_wait**
- **spr_star**
- **bg_1**

The origin of all of the sprites is middle center, except for **bg_1**, which has a default setting of top left.

There are two sounds, **snd_match** and **snd_no_match**, which can be added now.

There are three scripts. The first is **scr_check_match** with code that checks for matches to the left and right, and up and down, to see if there is a match. If there is a match, that object's id is saved to a **ds_list** for use later.

```
/// @function scr_check_match
if global.on_path exit;
if global.moving exit;
ds_list_clear(global.match_list);
ds_list_clear(global.match_3);
```

© Ben Tyers 2018

B. Tyers, *Practical GameMaker Projects*, https://doi.org/10.1007/978-1-4842-3745-8_9

```
//check left and right
with (obj_block)
{
    var a=instance_position(x,y,obj_block);
    var b=instance_position(x-32,y,obj_block);
    var c=instance_position(x+32,y,obj_block);
    if a!=noone && b!=noone && c!=noone
    if a.image_index==b.image_index && a.image_index==c.image_index
    {
        show_debug_message("Match has been found - left right");
        //add to ds list
        ds_list_add(global.match_list,a,b,c); //for destroying
        ds_list_add(global.match_3,a); //for star effect
    }
    else
    {
        show_debug_message("Noooooo has been found - left right");
        show_debug_message(string(a));
        show_debug_message(string(b));
        show_debug_message(string(c));
    }
}
//check up and down
with (obj_block)
{
    var a=instance_position(x,y,obj_block);
    var b=instance_position(x,y-32,obj_block);
    var c=instance_position(x,y+32,obj_block);
    if a!=noone && b!=noone && c!=noone
    if a.image_index==b.image_index && a.image_index==c.image_index
    {
```

```
        show_debug_message("Match has been found - up down");
        //add to ds list
        ds_list_add(global.match_list,a,b,c);//for destroying
        ds_list_add(global.match_3,a);//for star effect
    }
    else
    {
        show_debug_message("No match has been found - up down");
        show_debug_message(string(a));
        show_debug_message(string(b));
        show_debug_message(string(c));
    }
}

if ds_list_empty(global.match_list)
{
    if !global.match && global.this_block!=noone && global.other_block!=noone
    {
            audio_play_sound(snd_no_match,0,false);
            //move back
            global.other_block.x=global.first_x;
            global.other_block.y=global.first_y;
            global.this_block.x=global.second_x;
            global.this_block.y=global.second_y;
            //set back to noone
            global.this_block=noone;
            global.other_block=noone;
            //show_message("Inner Block");
    }

}
else audio_play_sound(snd_match,0,false);

global.this_block=noone;
global.other_block=noone;
if ds_list_size(global.match_list)==0 return false; else return true;
```

Next is **scr_move_blocks** with code to make the instances swap places using a path:

```
/// @function scr_move_blocks(first,second);
alarm[0]=room_speed*3; //for testing and make slow
show_debug_message("first id="+string(argument0));
show_debug_message("second id="+string(argument1));
var my_startx=x;
var my_starty=y;
global.first_x=argument0.x;
global.first_y=argument0.y;
global.second_x=argument1.x;
global.second_y=argument1.y;
if argument0=id
{
    global.this_block=id;
    global.other_block=argument1;
}
else
{
    global.this_block=argument1;
    global.other_block=argument0;
}
if global.this_block==noone
{
    show_debug_message("Not Selected ID");
    exit;
}
global.on_path=true;
//set depth
if id==global.this_block or id==global.other_block
{
    depth=-10;
}
{
    depth=-1;
}
```

```
if global.this_block==id
    {
    //move the blocks to target
            path_add_point(path,global.second_x,global.second_y,5);
            path_add_point(path,global.second_x-50,global.second_y,5);
            path_add_point(path,global.first_x,global.first_y,5);
            path_set_kind(path,true);
            path_set_closed(path,false);
            path_start(path,50,path_action_stop,true);

            with (global.other_block)
            {
                path_add_point(path,global.first_x,global.first_y,5);
                path_add_point(path,global.first_x+50,global.first_y,5);
                path_add_point(path,global.second_x,global.second_y,5);
                path_set_kind(path,true);
                path_set_closed(path,false);
                path_start(path,50,path_action_stop,true);
            }
    }
```

And finally **scr_check_to_drop** has code to check for empty spaces at the top of the sweets grid, creating a new instance if there is a free space:

```
/// @function scr_check_to_drop
if global.on_path exit;
for (var i=1; i<21; i+= 1)
{
        if collision_rectangle(88+size*i,0,72+size*i,116,obj_block, false,
        false )==noone
        {
            instance_create_layer(80+size*i,10,"Instances",obj_block);
            show_debug_message("Intance Created");
            global.moving=true;
            alarm[0]=room_speed;
        }
}
```

There is one font, **font_info**, which is Comic Sans size 24.

The first object is **obj_border**. Assign it sprite **spr_border** and uncheck the Visible setting.

Next is **obj_star**. Assign it **spr_star**. The instances of this object have their own layer named Star, which is the top layer. Add a **Create Event** with the following code:

```
/// @description Set Up
alarm[0]=room_speed*3;
scale=0.02;
```

Add a **Step Event** that increases and tests the value of scale:

```
/// @description increase scale
scale+=0.02;
image_angle++;
if scale=1 instance_destroy();
```

Add an **Alarm 0 Event** with the following code:

```
/// @description Destroy
instance_destroy();
```

Add a **Draw Event** with the following code:

```
/// @description Set Scale and Alpha
image_alpha=1-scale;
image_xscale=scale;
image_yscale=scale;
draw_self();
image_alpha=1;
```

Next is **obj_control**. There is no sprite for this object.

Add a **Create Event** with the following code:

```
/// @description Set Up & Create Play Ares
global.is_selected1=noone;
global.is_selected2=noone;
global.this_block=noone;
```

```
global.other_block=noone;
global.match=false;
global.match_list=ds_list_create();
global.match_3=ds_list_create();
level=6;
score=0;
size=32; //size of sprite dimensions

for (var i = 1; i < 21; i += 1)
{
    for (var j = 1; j < 18; j += 1)
    {
        instance_create_layer(80+size*i,j*size,"Instances",obj_block);
    }
}
//set mmoving flag
global.moving=true;
alarm[0]=room_speed;

random_set_seed(1);
```

Add a **Step Event** with the following code:

```
//set incase moving back
scr_check_to_drop();
```

Add an **Alarm 0 Event** with the following code:

```
// @description No more moving
show_debug_message("No more movement");
global.moving=false;
global.is_selected1=noone;
global.is_selected2=noone;

//destoy instance
show_debug_message("List Size"+string(ds_list_size(global.match_list)));
scr_check_match();
```

```
///create star effect
for (var i = 0; i < ds_list_size(global.match_3); i += 1)
{
    instance_create_layer(global.match_3[|i].x,global.match_3[|i].y,
    "Star",obj_star);
}
///create colour effect
for (var i = 0; i < ds_list_size(global.match_list); i += 1)
    {
        if instance_exists(global.match_list[|i])//check if not destroyed already
        //if present make effect in matching colour
        {
            switch global.match_list[|i].image_index
            {
                case 0:
                my_colour=c_red;
                break;
                case 1:
                my_colour=c_yellow;
                break;
                case 2:
                my_colour=c_blue;
                break;
                case 3:
                my_colour=c_green;
                break;
                case 4:
                my_colour=c_aqua;
                break;
                case 5:
                my_colour=c_maroon;
                break;
                case 6:
                my_colour=c_purple;
                break;
            }
```

```
        //create effects in colour
        effect_create_above(ef_firework,global.match_list[|i].x,global.
        match_list[|i].y,5,my_colour);
        effect_create_above(ef_flare,global.match_list[|i].x,global.
        match_list[|i].y,5,my_colour);
        effect_create_above(ef_spark,global.match_list[|i].x,global.
        match_list[|i].y,5,my_colour);
        effect_create_above(ef_star,global.match_list[|i].x,global.
        match_list[|i].y,5,my_colour);
        ///add score
        score+=10;

        }
    with (global.match_list[|i]) instance_destroy();
    }

if scr_check_match()
{
    global.moving=true;
    alarm[0]=room_speed*1;
}
```

Add a **Draw Event** with the following code:

```
/// @description Draw Info

//draw hud

draw_set_font(font_info);
draw_set_halign(fa_center);
draw_set_valign(fa_middle);
draw_set_colour(c_black);
draw_text(910,271,score);
draw_text(910,450,level);
if global.moving
{
    draw_sprite(spr_please_wait,0,room_width/2,706);
}
```

```
else
{
    draw_sprite(spr_make_move,0,room_width/2,706);
}
```

And finally add a **Key Press R Event** with the following code:

```
/// @description For Testing
game_restart();
```

The final object is **obj_block**. Assign it **spr_block**.

Add a **Create Event** with the following code:

```
/// @description Set a random image && Set Path
image_speed=0;
image_index=irandom(6);
path=path_add();
global.on_path=false;
global.moving=true;
alarm[0]=room_speed*2; //allow time for start blocks to drop
```

Add a **Step Event** with the following code:

```
/// @description Movement
///general movement
if global.on_path exit;
if !place_meeting(x,y+2,obj_border)
{
        y+=2;//make block fall
        global.moving=true;
        obj_control.alarm[0]=room_speed;
}

//show if selected
if global.is_selected1==id && !global.moving or global.is_selected2==id && (
{
        effect_create_above(ef_spark,x,y,1,c_white);
}
```

Add an **Alarm 0 Event** with the following code:

```
/// @description
global.on_path=false;
```

Add a **Left Pressed Event** with the following code:

```
/// @description check if selected or not
//prevent selection if moving
if global.moving
{
    global.is_selected1=noone;
    global.is_selected2=noone;
    exit;
}
//deselect if selected
if global.is_selected1==id
{
    global.is_selected1=noone;
    exit;
}
if global.is_selected1==noone
{
    global.is_selected1=id;
}
//allow second seleection if id different
else if global.is_selected2==noone && global.is_selected1!=id
{
    global.is_selected2=id;
}
if global.is_selected2!=noone && global.is_selected1!=noone
{
    with (global.is_selected1)
    {
        if distance_to_object(global.is_selected2)>1
        {
```

```
            global.is_selected2=noone;
            global.is_selected1=noone;
        }
    }
}
//check if ok
if global.is_selected2!=noone && global.is_selected1!=noone
{
    show_debug_message("Two Valid Blocks Selected");
    global.moving=true;
    obj_control.alarm[0]=room_speed*2;//allow to time to move and_check
    scr_move_blocks(global.is_selected1,global.is_selected2);
}
else
{
    show_debug_message("No Valid Blocks Selected");
}
```

Add a **Path Ended Event** with the following code:

```
/// @description allign ane check for mach
move_snap(16,16);
path_clear_points(path);
global.on_path=false;
global.moving=true;
obj_control.alarm[0]=room_speed; //allow time for local alarm to trigger
alarm[0]=room_speed;
```

Finally, add the following code to a **Clean Up Event** in **obj_control**:

```
/// @description Clear path from memory
path_delete(path);
```

Set up a single room named **room_game** to a size of 1024 x 768. Set the background as **bg_1**.

The final step is to create a new Instances layer named Star, as shown in Figure 9-1.

Figure 9-1. *The room setup*

Add one instance of **obj_control** and one of **obj_border**, which has been stretched as shown in Figure 9-1. This is achieved by placing an instance and then hovering over a corner and clicking and dragging it.

Figure 9-2 shows this game in action.

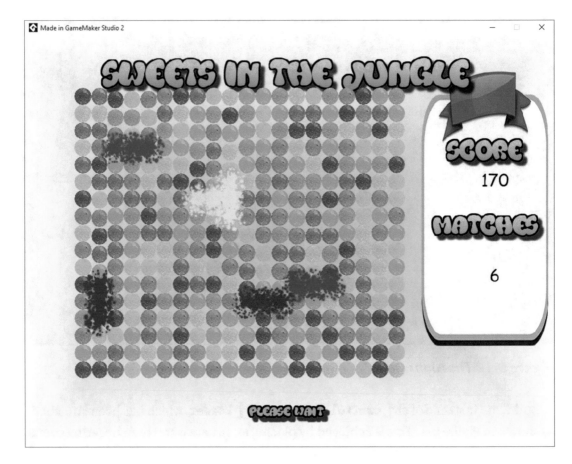

Figure 9-2. *The game in action*

A project file for the completed game is in the Resources folder.

EXTRA IDEAS FOR YOU TO TRY

1. Make it so the initial game setup does not start with matches present.

2. Create extra bonus effects if the player matches four or four in a row.

3. Make the pieces twice as big, and change the game code to reflect this.

4. Make it so a 2 x 2 grid of sweets also counts as a match.

5. Make a bonus object if the player makes a match of five sweets. If the player then matches three bonus objects, award a lot of points and create audio and visual effects.

CHAPTER 10

Tower Defense

This final game will put into practice everything you have learned so far, plus it will introduce a few more elements.

In this game, you will shoot and damage the enemy from turrets. You can place, buy, sell, and upgrade the turrets.

So that you can test the game at various points, you will start by creating the rooms. They are

- **room_splash**

- **room_start**

- **room_level_1**

- **room_level_2**

- **room_level_3**

- **room_level_4**

- **room_win**

- **room_gameover**

All of the rooms are 800 x 800 in size.

This game makes use of five scripts. The first is **scr_menu_info**, which sets the sub-image and draws text depending on whether player has enough cash:

```
/// @function scr_menu_info()
if available
{
    image_index=1;
}
```

© Ben Tyers 2018
B. Tyers, *Practical GameMaker Projects*, https://doi.org/10.1007/978-1-4842-3745-8_10

```
else
{
    image_index=0;
}
draw_self();
scr_text(center,y+45,"Cost: $"+string(price),c_white);

if available
{
    scr_text(center,y+80,"Available",c_white);
}
else
{

    scr_text(center,y+80,"Not Available",c_red);
}
```

The next is **scr_message**, which adds a message to a list:

```
//add message to a ds list
ds_list_add(global.message,argument0);
```

The next is **scr_angle_rotate**, which slowly moves between two angles at a given speed:

```
/// @function scr_angle_rotate(angle1,angle2,speed)
return argument0 + clamp(angle_difference(argument1, argument0), -argument2, argument2)
```

The next is **scr_sound**, which plays a given sound:

```
/// @function scr_sound(sound)
audio_play_sound(argument0,10,false);
```

And finally, **scr_text** draws text at given location and color:

```
/// @function scr_text(x,y,text,colour)
draw_set_colour(c_white);
draw_set_halign(fa_center);
draw_set_valign(fa_middle);
```

```
draw_set_colour(c_black);
draw_text(argument0-1,argument1-1,argument2);
draw_set_colour(argument3);
draw_text(argument0,argument1,argument2);
```

Now, go ahead and load in **snd_music** from the resources.

The first object is **obj_splash**. Add a **Create Event** that sets initial variables and loads any saved data:

```
/// @description Set Globals
global.sound=true;
global.message=ds_list_create();
lives=20;
ini_open("save.ini");
global.level=ini_read_real("save", "level", 1);
global.cash=ini_read_real("save", "cash", 800);
ini_close();
//testing
global.cash=20000;
///Go To Menu
room_goto(room_start);
```

Next up is **obj_level_parent**. Add a **Step Event** that sets whether the level is locked or unlocked:

```
if my_id>=global.level
{
    unlocked=true;
}
else
{
    unlocked=false;
}
```

Add a **Left Released Event** with GML to take the player to the appropriate game level room:

```
/// @description Go to room if unlocked
if unlocked
{
    switch (my_id)
    {
    case 1:
        room_goto(room_level_1);
        break;
    case 2:
        room_goto(room_level_2);
        break;
    case 3:
        room_goto(room_level_3);
        break;
    case 4:
        room_goto(room_level_4);
        break;
    }
}
```

Add a **Draw Event** with the following code:

```
draw_self();
scr_text(x,y,my_id,c_red);
```

Next up is **obj_level_1_button**. Assign it **spr_button**, set the origin as middle center, and set **obj_level_parent** as its parent. Add a **Create Event** with the following code:

```
///Set Up
my_id=1;
unlocked=false;
```

Next, create **obj_level_2_button**, **obj_level_3_button**, and **obj_level_4_button**, changing **my_id** to 2, 3, and 4, accordingly.

Next, create an object named **obj_menu_control** with the following **Create Event** code:

```
/// @description Play Music
if audio_is_playing(snd_music) audio_stop_sound(snd_music);
audio_play_sound(snd_music,0,true);
```

Next, create a group in objects section of the Resources tree and name it "Splash and Menu" and then move the objects into this group folder.

Open **room_splash** and place one instance of **obj_splash** in it.

Open **room_start** and place one instance each of the level buttons and one of **obj_menu_control**.

Next, you'll design a level. Go ahead and load in **spr_tile**. Then, in the Resources tree, right-click tilesets and add a new tile called **bg_tiles** and select the sprite **spr_tile** you just created. Click Tile Set Properties and set the tile width and height as 32 and output border x and y as 2, as shown in Figure 10-1.

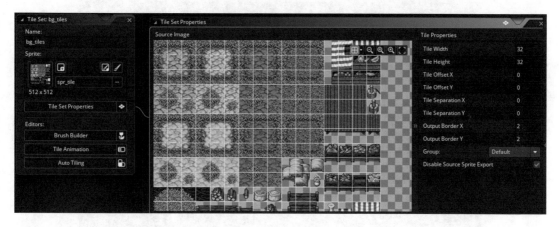

Figure 10-1. *Setting the tile properties*

Open **room_level_1** and add a tile layer, as shown in Figure 10-2.

Figure 10-2. *Adding a tile layer*

Select the tile layer and then choose the tileset you just created, as shown in Figure 10-3.

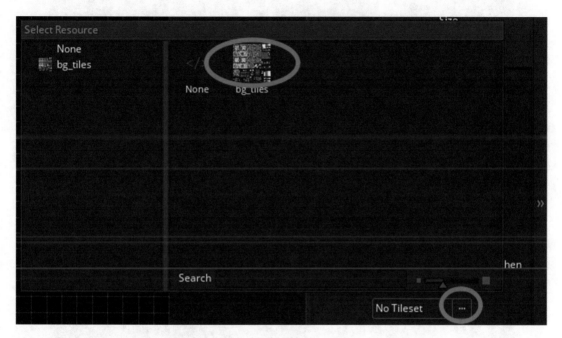

Figure 10-3. *Choosing the newly created tileset*

You can now select parts of the tile and place them in the room. Tip: Hold down the Shift key to place multiple tiles.

Design the level as shown in Figure 10-4.

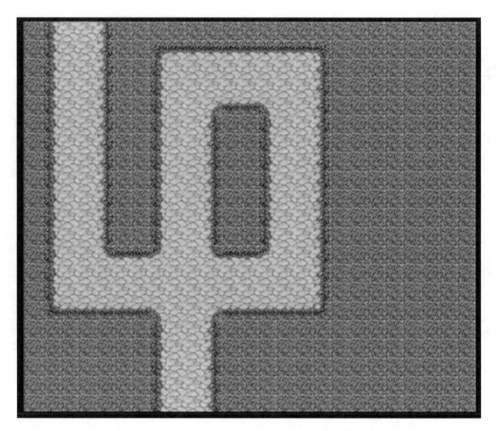

Figure 10-4. *The level's layout*

Next, load in the remaining sounds:

- **snd_beep**
- **snd_missile_launch**
- **snd_bullet_1**
- **snd_bullet_2**
- **snd_hit**
- **snd_die_1**
- **snd_die_2**
- **snd_die_3**

- **snd_die_4**

- **snd_weapon_selected**

- **snd_not_enough_cash**

- **snd_you_are_dead**

- **snd_level_1**

Next, you'll create a path for the enemy to follow. Open up **room_level_1** and create a **Path Layer**. Make a new path called **path_level_1**, as shown in Figure 10-5. Note that the start and end points are outside the room.

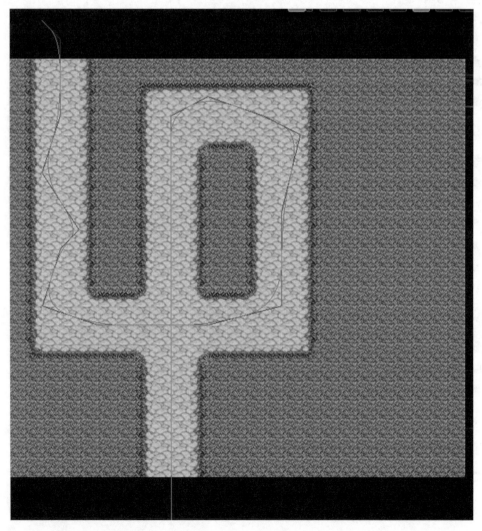

Figure 10-5. *Showing the path setup*

Next, create an object named **obj_level_1_control** and add the following **Create Event** code to set the wave settings and queue some messages:

```
/// @description Set Up
global.wave=1;
total_waves=10;
zombie_count=0;
global.zombies_killed=0;
global.message="";
scr_message("Messages Will Appear Here");
scr_message("Click To Select Available Towers");
scr_message("Place On Empty Foundations");
scr_message("Right Click To Upgrade");
scr_message("Left Click To Sell");
alarm[1]=room_speed*5;
scr_sound(snd_level_1);
```

Add an **Alarm 1 Event** with the following code:

```
/// @description spawn zombie
if zombie_count<10
{
    instance_create_layer(x,y,"Instances",obj_enemy_1);
    alarm[1]=room_speed*2;
    zombie_count++;
}
```

Add an **Alarm 2 Event** with the following code:

```
/// @description Next Wave
global.wave+=1;
alarm[1]=room_speed;
```

Add a **Step Event** with the following code:

```
/// @description Level Control
if lives<=0
{
    room_goto(room_gameover);
}
```

```
if zombie_count==10 && global.zombies_killed==10
{
    instance_create_layer(250,400,"Instances",obj_level_complete);
    zombie_count=0;
    global.zombies_killed=0;
    alarm[2]=room_speed;
    //destroy any bullets or missiles on screen
    if instance_exists(obj_bullet_parent) with (obj_bullet_parent)
    instance_destroy();
    if instance_exists(obj_missile) with (obj_missile) instance_destroy();
}
if global.wave==11
{
    instance_create_layer(400,400,"Instances",obj_level_complete);
    if global.level==3 global.level=4;
    if global.level==2 global.level=3;
    if global.level==1 global.level=2;
    ini_open("save.ini");
    ini_write_real("save", "level", global.level);
    ini_write_real("save", "cash", global.cash);
    ini_close();
    room_goto(room_win);

}
```

And add a **Draw Event** with the following code:

```
/// @description Draw Wave Info
draw_sprite(spr_info_bg,0,x,y);
scr_text(x+60,y,"LEVEL"+string(global.wave)+"0f"+string(total_waves),
c_white);
```

That is all for this object.

Next is **obj_enemy_1**. Assign it the sprite named **spr_enemy** from the Resources folder.

Add the following **Create Event** code:

```
///Start On A Path
path_start(path_level_1,2,path_action_restart,true); hp=1000*global.wave;
max_hp=1000*global.wave;
```

Add a **Step Event** with the following code:

```
/// @description Point in direction and Check hp
image_angle=direction;
///Check if Dead
if hp<0
{
    scr_sound(snd_die_1);
    instance_create_layer(x,y,"Instances",obj_blood_splatter);
    instance_destroy();
    global.zombies_killed+=1;
    global.cash+=50*global.wave;
}
```

Add a **Draw Event** to draw the enemy and a mini healthbar above:

```
/// @description Draw Self & Healthbar
draw_self();
draw_healthbar(x-25,y-25,x+25,y-22,(hp/max_hp)*100,c_red,c_black,
c_green,0,true,true);
```

Add a **Path Ended Event** with the following code:

```
/// @description Reduce Player lives
lives-=1;
```

Add a **Collision Event** with **obj_missile** with the following code:

```
/// @description Destroy if Hit by Targeted Missile
if other.target==id
{
    hp-=other.strength;
    instance_create_layer(x,y,"Instances",obj_blood_splatter);
    with (other) instance_destroy();
```

```
    scr_sound(snd_hit);
}
```

Add a **Collision Event** with **obj_bullet_parent** with the following GML:

```
/// @description Reduce HP if hit by bullet
hp-=other.strength;
instance_create_layer(x,y,obj_blood_splatter);
scr_sound(snd_hit);
with (other) instance_destroy();
```

Next is **obj_blood_splatter**. Assign it the sprite strip **spr_blood_1** and set the origin as 32 x 34.

Add a **Create Event** with the following code:

```
/// @description Set animation speed
image_speed=0.5;
```

Add an **Animation End Event** with the following code:

```
/// @description Destroy
instance_destroy();
```

Add a **Draw Event** with the following code:

```
/// @description Draw spread out
for (var i=1; i<7; i+= 1)
{
    draw_sprite_ext(sprite_index,image_index,x,y,1,1,i*60,c_white,1);
}
```

Next is **obj_level_complete**; assign it **spr_level_complete**. Add the following **Create Event** code:

```
/// @description Set Alarm
alarm[0]=room_speed*2;
```

Add an **Alarm 0 Event** with this code:

```
/// @description Destroy
instance_destroy();
```

Finally, make sure the room layers for **room_level_1** are in the order shown in Figure 10-6.

Figure 10-6. *Room layers in order*

Next, you'll create some weapons and some turrets to fire the weapons from.

First, create an object named **obj_bullet_parent**. There is no code or sprite for this object.

Next up is **obj_bullet**. Assign it **spr_bullet_1** and set the origin as center. Add the following **Create Event** code:

```
/// @description Play audio
scr_sound(snd_bullet_1);
```

Add a **Step Event** with code that destroys itself if outside the range of the turret:

```
/// @description Destroy
if distance_to_object(source)>range instance_destroy();
```

Its parent is **obj_bullet_parent**.

Next is **obj_bullet_2**. Assign it **spr_bullet_2** and set the origin to center.

Add a **Create Event** with the following code:

```
scr_sound(snd_bullet_2);
```

Add a **Step Event** that destroys itself if outside range:

```
/// @description Destroy
if distance_to_object(source)>range instance_destroy();
```

Set **obj_bullet_parent** as its parent.

Next is **obj_missile**. Assign it **spr_missile**, which consists of two images, and set the origin to 36 x 8.

Add a **Create Event** with the following code:

```
/// @description Set Up
live=true;
active=true;
alarm[0]=room_speed*5;
scr_sound(snd_missile_launch);
```

Add a **Step Event** that checks whether the target is still present; if not, it looks for the nearest enemy and makes a new target:

```
/// @description Look For Target
if !instance_exists(target) && instance_exists(obj_enemy_1)
{
    target=instance_nearest(x,y,obj_enemy_1);
}
///track target
if instance_exists(target)
{
    tx = target.x;
    ty = target.y;
    direction = scr_angle_rotate(direction, point_direction(x, y, tx, ty), 5);
    image_angle = direction;
}
```

That is all for this object.

Next is **obj_flash**. Assign it the sprite strip **spr_flash** and set the origin to 91 x 32.

Add an **Animation End Event** with the following code:

```
instance_destroy();
```

That is all for this object.

Next is **obj_tower_parent**; it does not have a sprite.

Add a **Mouse Left Released Event** with the following code:

```
/// @description Sell
global.cash+=sell;
instance_create_layer(x,y,"Instances",obj_place);
instance_destroy();
```

Add a **Mouse Right Released Event** with GML that upgrades if available and if the player has enough cash to upgrade:

```
/// @description  Upgrade
obj_buyer.selected=0;
if global.cash>=upgrade && level<2
{
    level+=1;
    global.cash-=upgrade;
    range+=range/3;
}
```

Add a **Draw Event** with the following code:

```
draw_sprite(spr_place,0,x,y);
draw_self();
```

Add a **Draw GUI Event** with the following code, which draws the current level and shows the turret's range as a red circle and whether the turret can be upgraded:

```
/// @description Draw Info
if position_meeting(mouse_x,mouse_y,id)
{
    scr_text(x,y,"Level="+string(level),c_white);
    draw_set_alpha(0.4);
    draw_set_colour(c_red);
    draw_circle(x,y,range,false);
    draw_set_alpha(1);
    scr_text(x,y,"Level="+string(level),c_white);
    if level<2 && global.cash>=upgrade
    {
```

```
        scr_text(x,y-40,"Right Click To Upgrade",c_white);
    }
    scr_text(x,y+40,"Left Click To Sell For $"+string(sell),c_white);
}
```

Next up is **obj_turret_1**. Assign it **spr_turret_1**, set the origin to 45 x 47, and set the parent as **obj_tower_parent**.

Add the following **Create Event** code:

```
/// @description Set Up
level=0;
range=100;
target=noone;
upgrade=50;
sell=0;
```

Add a **Step Event** with the following code:

```
/// @description Do Various Thyings
///set sub image
image_index=level;
///Look For Target - if destroyed find another
if instance_exists(obj_enemy_1)
{
    target=instance_nearest(x,y,obj_enemy_1);
    if alarm[0]==-1 alarm[0]=room_speed+irandom(10); //for bullet
    if distance_to_object(target)<range
    {
        target=instance_nearest(x,y,obj_enemy_1)
        tx = target.x;
        ty = target.y;
    direction = scr_angle_rotate(direction, point_direction(x, y, tx, ty), 5);
    image_angle = direction;
    }
}
```

```
///Set Selling Price:
sell=floor(((level+1)*upgrade)/2);
```

Add an **Alarm 0 Event** that creates bullet(s) when the alarm triggers:

```
/// @description Create Bullet If Target in Range
if distance_to_object(target)<range
{
    if level==0
    {
        var bullet=instance_create_layer(x+lengthdir_x(30, image_angle),
        y+lengthdir_y(30, image_angle),"Front",obj_bullet_1);
        bullet.image_angle=direction;
        bullet.direction=direction;
        bullet.speed=6;
        bullet.source=id;
        bullet.range=range;
        bullet.strength=50+(level*50);
        var flash=instance_create_layer(x+lengthdir_x(30, image_angle),
        y+lengthdir_y(30, image_angle),"Front",obj_flash);
        flash.image_angle=direction;
    }
    if level==1
    {
        //first bullet & flash
        var bullet=instance_create_layer(x+lengthdir_x(35, image_angle)+
        lengthdir_x(9, image_angle - 90),y+lengthdir_y(35, image_angle)+
        lengthdir_y(9, image_angle - 90),"Front",obj_bullet_1);
        bullet.image_angle=direction;
        bullet.direction=direction;
        bullet.speed=6;
        bullet.source=id;
        bullet.range=range;
        bullet.strength=50+(level*50);
```

```
    var flash=instance_create_layer(x+lengthdir_x(35, image_angle)+
    lengthdir_x(9, image_angle - 90),y+lengthdir_y(35, image_angle)+
    lengthdir_y(9, image_angle - 90),"Front",obj_flash);
    flash.image_angle=direction;
    //second bullet & flash
    var bullet=instance_create_layer(x+lengthdir_x(35, image_angle)+
    lengthdir_x(-9, image_angle - 90),y+lengthdir_y(35, image_angle)+
    lengthdir_y(-9, image_angle - 90),"Front",obj_bullet_1);
    bullet.image_angle=direction;
    bullet.direction=direction;
    bullet.speed=6;
    bullet.source=id;
    bullet.range=range;
    bullet.strength=50+(level*50);
    var flash=instance_create_layer(x+lengthdir_x(35, image_angle)+
    lengthdir_x(-9, image_angle - 90),y+lengthdir_y(35, image_angle)+
    lengthdir_y(-9, image_angle - 90),"Front",obj_flash);
    flash.image_angle=direction;
}
if level==2
{
    var bullet=instance_create_layer(x+lengthdir_x(30, image_angle),
    y+lengthdir_y(30, image_angle),"Front",obj_bullet_1);
    bullet.image_angle=direction;
    bullet.direction=direction;
    bullet.speed=6;
    bullet.source=id;
    bullet.range=range;
    bullet.strength=50+(level*50);
    var flash=instance_create_layer(x+lengthdir_x(30, image_angle),
    y+lengthdir_y(30, image_angle),"Front",obj_flash);
    flash.image_angle=direction;
}
}
```

That is all for this object.

Create an object named **obj_place** and assign to it, with the origin as center, **spr_place**.

To enable testing at this stage, create an object named **obj_buyer**. No sprite or code is needed right now, but you will come back to it later. Place one instance of **obj_buyer** in **room_level_1**.

Place a few instances of **obj_turret_1** on the grass areas of **room_level_1**.

Next, create the other two types of towers.

The first is **obj_turret_2**. Assign it sprite strip **spr_tower_2** and set the origin as middle center.

Add the following **Create Event** code:

```
///Set Up
level=0;
range=200;
target=noone;
upgrade=250;
sell=0;
```

Add an **Alarm 0 Event** with the following code:

```
/// @description Look For Target
if distance_to_object(target)<range
{
    if level==0
    {
        var bullet=instance_create_layer(x+lengthdir_x(30, image_angle),
        y+lengthdir_y(30, image_angle),"Instances",obj_bullet_2);
        bullet.image_angle=direction;
        bullet.direction=direction;
        bullet.speed=6;
        bullet.source=id;
        bullet.range=range;
        bullet.strength=50+(level*100);
        var flash=instance_create_layer(x+lengthdir_x(30, image_angle),
        y+lengthdir_y(30, image_angle),"Instances",obj_flash);
        flash.image_angle=direction;
    }
```

```
if level==1
{
    //Create Bullet & Flash 1
    var bullet=instance_create_layer(x+lengthdir_x(35, image_angle)+
    lengthdir_x(9, image_angle - 90),y+lengthdir_y(35, image_angle)+
    lengthdir_y(9, image_angle - 90),"Instances",obj_bullet_2);
    bullet.image_angle=direction;
    bullet.direction=direction;
    bullet.speed=6;
    bullet.source=id;
    bullet.range=range;
    bullet.strength=50+(level*100);
    var flash=instance_create_layer(x+lengthdir_x(35, image_angle)+
    lengthdir_x(9, image_angle - 90),y+lengthdir_y(35, image_angle)+
    lengthdir_y(9, image_angle - 90),"Instances",obj_flash);
    flash.image_angle=direction;
    //Create Bullet & Flash 2
    var bullet=instance_create_layer(x+lengthdir_x(35, image_angle)+
    lengthdir_x(-9, image_angle - 90),y+lengthdir_y(35, image_angle)+
    lengthdir_y(-9, image_angle - 90),"Instances",obj_bullet_2);
    bullet.image_angle=direction;
    bullet.direction=direction;
    bullet.speed=6;
    bullet.source=id;
    bullet.range=range;
    bullet.strength=50+(level*100);
    var flash=instance_create_layer(x+lengthdir_x(35, image_angle)+
    lengthdir_x(-9, image_angle - 90),y+lengthdir_y(35, image_angle)+
    lengthdir_y(-9, image_angle - 90),"Instances",obj_flash);
    flash.image_angle=direction;
}
 if level==2
 {
```

```
        var bullet=instance_create_layer(x+lengthdir_x(30, image_angle),
        y+lengthdir_y(30, image_angle),"Instances",obj_bullet_2);
        bullet.image_angle=direction;
        bullet.direction=direction;
        bullet.speed=6;
        bullet.source=id;
        bullet.range=range;
        bullet.strength=50+(level*100);
        var flash=instance_create_layer(x+lengthdir_x(30, image_angle),
        y+lengthdir_y(30, image_angle),"Instances",obj_flash);
        flash.image_angle=direction;
    }

}
```

Add a **Step Event** with the following code:

```
/// @description Various Checks
///set sub image
image_index=level;
///Look For Target - if destroyed find another
if instance_exists(obj_enemy_1)
{
    target=instance_nearest(x,y,obj_enemy_1);
    if alarm[0]==-1 alarm[0]=room_speed+irandom(10);//for bullet
}
///Set Moving Direction Angle
if instance_exists(obj_enemy_1) && distance_to_object(target)<range
{
    target=instance_nearest(x,y,obj_enemy_1)
    var tx = target.x;
    var ty = target.y;
    direction = scr_angle_rotate(direction, point_direction(x, y, tx, ty), 8);
    image_angle = direction;
}
```

```
///Set Selling Price:
sell=floor(((level+1)*upgrade)/2);
```

Set the parent as **obj_tower_parent**.

Next is **obj_turret_3**. Assign it the sprite strip **spr_turret_3** and set the origin as middle center.

Add a **Create Event** with the following code:

```
/// @description Set Up
level=0;
range=250;
target=noone;
reload_speed=2;
upgrade=1000;
sell=0;
```

Add an **Alarm 0 Event** that creates missile(s) depending on the turret's level and whether there is an enemy in range:

```
/// @description Look For Target
if distance_to_object(target)<range
{
    if level==0
    {
        var missile=instance_create_layer(x+lengthdir_x(30, image_angle),
        y+lengthdir_y(30, image_angle),"Front",obj_missile);
        missile.image_angle=direction;
        missile.direction=direction;
        missile.speed=6;
        missile.source=id;
        missile.range=range;
        missile.strength=250+(level*100);
        missile.target=target;
        var flash=instance_create_layer(x+lengthdir_x(30, image_angle),
        y+lengthdir_y(30, image_angle),"Front",obj_flash);
        flash.image_angle=direction;
```

```
    }
    if level==1
    {
        //Create First Missile & Flash
        var missile=instance_create_layer(x+lengthdir_x(35, image_angle)+
        lengthdir_x(9, image_angle - 90),y+lengthdir_y(35, image_angle)+
        lengthdir_y(9, image_angle - 90),"Front",obj_missile);
        missile.image_angle=direction;
        missile.direction=direction;
        missile.speed=6;
        missile.source=id;
        missile.range=range;
        missile.strength=250+(level*100);
        missile.target=target;
        var flash=instance_create_layer(x+lengthdir_x(35, image_angle)+
        lengthdir_x(9, image_angle - 90),y+lengthdir_y(35, image_angle)+
        lengthdir_y(9, image_angle - 90),"Front",obj_flash);
        flash.image_angle=direction;
        //Create Second Missile & Flash
        var missile=instance_create_layer(x+lengthdir_x(35, image_angle)+
        lengthdir_x(-9, image_angle - 90),y+lengthdir_y(35, image_angle)+
        lengthdir_y(-9, image_angle - 90),"Front",obj_missile);
        missile.image_angle=direction;
        missile.direction=direction;
        missile.speed=6;
        missile.source=id;
        missile.range=range;
        missile.strength=250+(level*100);
        missile.target=target;
        var flash=instance_create_layer(x+lengthdir_x(35, image_angle)+
        lengthdir_x(-9, image_angle - 90),y+lengthdir_y(35, image_angle)+
        lengthdir_y(-9, image_angle - 90),"Front",obj_flash);
        flash.image_angle=direction;
    }
```

```
if level==2
{
    var missile=instance_create_layer(x+lengthdir_x(30, image_angle),
    y+lengthdir_y(30, image_angle),"Front",obj_missile);
    missile.image_angle=direction;
    missile.direction=direction;
    missile.speed=6;
    missile.source=id;
    missile.range=range;
    missile.strength=250+(level*100);
    missile.target=target;
    var flash=instance_create_layer(x+lengthdir_x(30, image_angle),
    y+lengthdir_y(30, image_angle),"Front",obj_flash);
    flash.image_angle=direction;
}

}
```

Add a **Step Event** with the following code:

```
/// @description Various Steps
///set sub image
image_index=level;
///Look For Target - if destroyed find another
if instance_exists(obj_enemy_1)
{
    target=instance_nearest(x,y,obj_enemy_1);
    if alarm[0]==-1 alarm[0]=room_speed*reload_speed+irandom(10);//for bullet
    ///Set Moving Direction Angle
    if distance_to_object(target)<range
    {
        target=instance_nearest(x,y,obj_enemy_1)
        tx = target.x;
        ty = target.y;
        direction = scr_angle_rotate(direction, point_direction(x, y, tx, ty), 5);
        image_angle = direction;
    }
}
```

```
///Set Selling Price:
sell=floor(((level+1)*upgrade)/2);
```

Set the parent as **obj_tower_parent**.

Next, let's set up backgrounds for the other objects that you'll be using.

First, load in **spr_info_bg** and set the origin as 40 x 35.

Create an object named **obj_coin_hud** and set the sprite as **spr_info_bg**. Make a **Draw Event** and add the following code:

```
/// @description Draw Coin Hud
draw_self();
draw_sprite(spr_cash,0,x,y);
scr_text(x+100,y,global.cash,c_white);
```

Load in **spr_cash** with the origin as middle center.

Next, create an object named **obj_lives_hud** and assign it **spr_info_bg**. Add the following **Draw Event** code:

```
/// @description Draw Lives
draw_self();
draw_sprite(spr_lives,0,x,y);
scr_text(x+100,y,lives,c_white);
```

Load in **spr_lives** and set the origin as middle center.

Open up the **obj_level_1** control and assign it the sprite **spr_info_bg**. Change the **Draw Event** to

```
/// @description Draw Wave Info
draw_sprite(spr_info_bg,0,x,y);
scr_text(x,y,"LEVEL"+string(global.wave)+"Of"+string(total_waves),c_white);
```

Place one instance each of **obj_coin_hud**, **obj_lives_hud**, and **obj_level_1_control**, as shown in Figure 10-7.

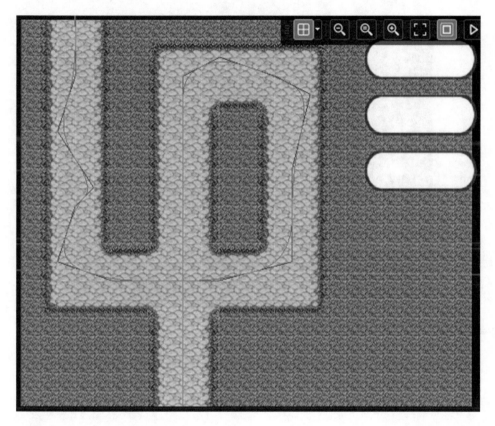

Figure 10-7. *Instances placed in room*

Next, open up **obj_room_level_1** and delete the tower instances you used for testing.

Create two instance layers, Front and Back, and set them in the order shown in Figure 10-8.

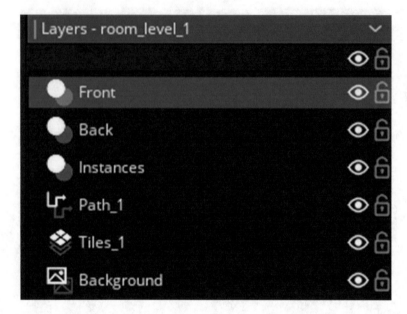

Figure 10-8. *New instance layers added*

Next, place instances of **obj_place** in all of the places where the player is allowed to build their turrets, as shown in Figure 10-9. Do this on the Back instances layer.

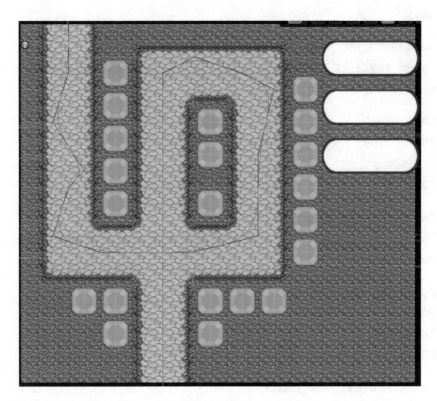

Figure 10-9. *obj_place instances placed in room*

Create a new object named **obj_menu_parent** and set the **Step Event** code as the following:

```
/// @description Draw If Available or Not
scr_menu_info();
```

Set the **Draw Event** GML as the following:

```
/// @description Draw If Available or Not
scr_menu_info();
```

Next, create an object named **obj_turret_1_menu**. Assign it the sprite **obj_turret_1_menu** and set the origin as center. Add the following **Create Event** code:

```
/// @description Set Up
price=50;
available=false;
center=680;
```

Set the parent as **obj_menu_parent**.

Next is **obj_turret_2_menu**. Assign it **spr_turret_2_menu**. Add the following **Create Event** code:

```
///Set Up
price=250;
available=false;
center=680;
```

Set the parent as **obj_menu_parent**.

Next is **obj_turret_3_menu**. Assign it **spr_turret_3_menu**. Add the following **Create Event** code:

```
/// @description Set Up
price=1000;
available=false;
center=680;
```

Set the parent to **obj_menu_parent**.

Place one instance of each of the three menu turrets in **room_level_1** as shown in Figure 10-10.

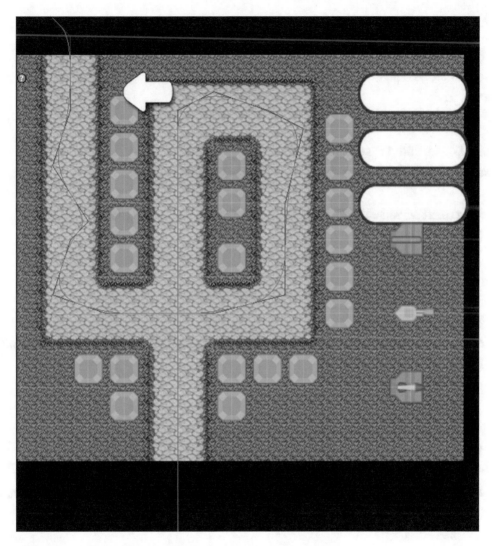

Figure 10-10. *Menu objects placed*

Next up is **obj_buyer**. Open it and assign the sprite **spr_arrow** to it with the origin at 12 x 12.

Add a **Create Event** with the following code:

```
/// @description Set Up
selected=0;
```

Add a **Step Event** with the following code:

```
/// @description Various Steps
///set at mouse pos
x=mouse_x;
y=mouse_y;

///set mouse and if selected
if mouse_check_button_released(mb_left) && selected==0
{
    if global.cash>=50 && position_meeting(x, y, obj_turret_1_menu)
    {
        selected=1;
        cost=50;
        scr_sound(snd_weapon_selected);
    }
    else if global.cash>=250 && position_meeting(x, y, obj_turret_2_menu)
    {
        selected=2;
        cost=250;
        scr_sound(snd_weapon_selected);
    }
///set if selected
    else if global.cash>=1000 && position_meeting(x, y, obj_turret_3_menu)
    {
        selected=3;
        cost=1000;
        scr_sound(snd_weapon_selected);
    }
    else scr_sound(snd_not_enough_cash);
}

///place grid if allowed
if selected>=1 && mouse_check_button_released(mb_left) && position_
meeting(x, y, obj_place)
{
```

```
    if selected==1
    {
        var nearest=instance_nearest(x,y,obj_place);
        instance_create_layer(nearest.x,nearest.y,"Back",obj_turret_1);
        global.cash-=cost;
        selected=0;
        with nearest instance_destroy();

    }
    if selected==2
    {
        var nearest=instance_nearest(x,y,obj_place);
        instance_create_layer(nearest.x,nearest.y,"Back",obj_turret_2);
        global.cash-=cost;
        selected=0;
        with nearest instance_destroy();

    }
    if selected==3
    {
        var nearest=instance_nearest(x,y,obj_place);
        instance_create_layer(nearest.x,nearest.y,"Back",obj_turret_3);
        global.cash-=cost;
        selected=0;
        with nearest instance_destroy();

    }
}
```

Add a **Right Mouse Button Released Event** with the following code:

```
///deselect
selected=0;
```

Add a **Draw Event** with the following code:

```
/// @description Set Sprite
if selected==1
{
    sprite_index=spr_turret_1;
}
else if selected==2
{
    sprite_index=spr_turret_2;
}
else if selected==3
{
    sprite_index=spr_turret_3;
}
else if selected==0
{
    sprite_index=spr_arrow;
}
image_speed=0;
draw_self();
scr_text(x,y,selected,c_white);
```

Place one instance of this object in **room_level_1** on the Front layer.

The final object is **obj_message**. Add this **Create Event** code:

```
/// @description set up
depth=-100;
can_show=true;
to_draw="";
x=400;
y=780;
```

Add an **Alarm 0 Event** with this code:

```
/// @description alarm0 set alarm1
alarm[1]=room_speed*1;
to_draw="";
```

Add an **Alarm 1 Event** with this code:

```
/// @description set as able to show
can_show=true;
```

Add a **Step Event** with this code:

```
/// @description check if message waiting
if !ds_list_empty(global.message) && can_show
{
    to_draw=ds_list_find_value(global.message,0);
    ds_list_delete(global.message,0);
    can_show=false;
    alarm[0]=room_speed*4;
}
```

Add a **Draw Event** with code that displays a current message if present:

```
/// @description draw message
if to_draw!=""
{
    scr_text(400,650,to_draw,c_blue);
}
```

That is all for this object. Open **room_level_1** and place an instance of this object on the Front layer.

Finally, let's do a bit of housekeeping so the bullets and missiles appear above other objects.

Open the **Alarm 0 Events** for objects **obj_turret_1**, **obj_turret_2**, and **obj_turret_3** and change the layer that the bullet and missile instances are being created on to the Front layer.

Next, create an object named **obj_gameover**. In a **Create Event**, add the following code:

```
/// @description Set Alarm
alarm[0]=room_speed*5;
scr_sound(snd_you_are_dead);
```

In an **Alarm 0 Event**, add this code:

```
/// @description Set Alarm
alarm[0]=room_speed*5;
scr_sound(snd_you_are_dead);
```

And in a **Draw Event**, add this code:

```
/// @description Draw
scr_text(room_width/2,room_height/2,"You Are Dead",c_white);
```

Place one instance of this object in **room_gameover**.

Finally, create an object named **obj_win** with this **Create Event** code:

```
/// @description Set Alarm
alarm[0]=room_speed*5;
```

Make an **Alarm 0 Event** with this code:

```
/// @description Restart
room_goto(room_start);
```

And make a **Draw Event** with the following code:

```
/// @description Draw
scr_text(room_width/2,room_height/2,"You Win",c_white);
```

Place one instance of this object in **room_win**.

Figure 10-11 shows this game in action.

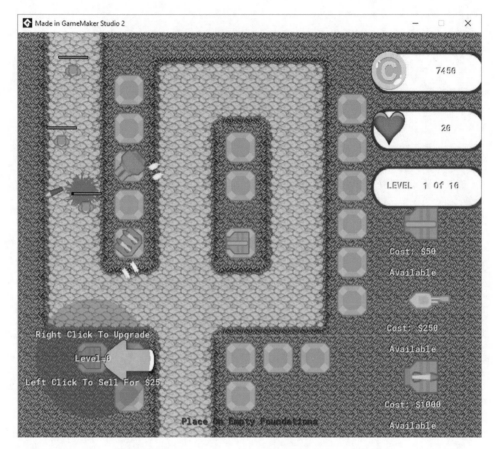

Figure 10-11. *The game in action*

A project file for the completed game is in the Resources folder. The additional rooms are present for you to design your own levels.

EXTRA IDEAS FOR YOU TO TRY

1. For each stage, use multiple paths with slight variations, getting the enemy to choose one at random when it starts moving.

2. Create a new weapon that drops nukes over the play area.

3. Make an enemy parent object, and allow easy integration of new enemies.

4. Design and set up three of your own stages. You can use the three level rooms that you created already.

5. Make a system that allows the player to create (and save) their own level designs.

Index

© Ben Tyers 2018
B. Tyers, *Practical GameMaker Projects*, https://doi.org/10.1007/978-1-4842-3745-8

Printed in the United States
By Bookmasters